"Salvation is a serious issue. Scripture commands us, on the one hand, to 'work out our salvation with fear and trembling' and, on the other, it paints beautiful pictures of believers walking in great assurance. J.D. helps us see what conversion really is and what it is not. This book will be a help for those who wrestle with their position before God and a wake-up call for those with false confidence. I recommend it highly."

—Matt Chandler, lead pastor, The Village Church,
and president, Acts 29 Church Planting Network

"Warmly personal. Immensely helpful. Wonderfully practical. Thoroughly biblical. I wholeheartedly recommend this book to every Christian who longs to know, experience, and spread assurance of salvation in Christ."

—David Platt, pastor,
The Church at Brook Hills, Birmingham, AL,
and author of New York Times bestselling *Radical*

"So much emphasis today is on the power of personal persuasion in sharing the gospel. What to say, how to say it. Reasons to believe, proofs for the authority of scripture, methods for gaining credibility blah blah blah. Pick up a copy of my friend J.D. Greear's book and learn the marks of a person saved by Jesus Christ. I commend it to you."

—Dr. James MacDonald, senior pastor,
Harvest Bible Chapel and author of *Vertical Church*

"Outstanding! This is a truly useful book. It's readable, engaging and packed with scriptural insight. It not only gives hope to Christians struggling with assurance of salvation, it will equip any Christian to better share the gospel and guide others toward genuine repentance and faith in Jesus."

—Joshua Harris, pastor and author of *Humble Orthodoxy*

"Don't let the provocative first half of the title scare you away from reading this important book! Emanating from his own personal and pastoral experience, yet with feet firmly planted in the sufficiency of Scripture, Greear is far more interested in helping us have genuine biblical assurance of salvation than anything else. He rightly reminds us we must emphasize the absolute indispensability of repentance and faith as necessary for salvation. Though I might quibble over a few things I would express differently, the vast majority of J.D.'s book I wholeheartedly endorse. Timely, engagingly written, and thoroughly practical, it deserves a place on every pastor's shelf. Buy it! Apply it!"

—Dr. David L. Allen, dean, School of Theology,
Southwestern Baptist Theological Seminary

"This is a very helpful and needed book. Untold numbers of people are thinking of themselves as true Christians when really theirs is a false assurance; while others are true Christians but lack a solid assurance. The book spells out how to teach the gospel in such a way as to help avoid these tragic results and how to help deliver those who are experiencing them. The emphasis on clear presentation of the meaning and evidence of repentance and faith is exactly what is needed. Also the difference a genuine assurance of salvation can make in one's life is brought out. I highly recommend this book!"

—Frank Barker, pastor emeritus,
Briarwood Presbyterian Church, Birmingham, AL

"A sensitive conscience can be a curse from Satan or a blessing from God. Does your conscience drive you from God, or to Him? In this book, J.D. Greear gets the gospel right. And the gospel is the way from conviction to salvation. This book should help you know how to place your conscience in the Lord's hands, where it can be a tool greatly used by God, as it was in Augustine's life, or Martin Luther's."

—Dr. Mark Dever, pastor
and author of *9 Marks of the Healthy Church*

"Every Christian struggles with doubts about salvation. The comforting passages of Scripture, assuring believers of their hope in salvation, were written to build up faith in the face of doubt. *Stop Asking Jesus Into Your Heart* guides readers through both assurance and perseverance in a life-altering way. Greear's work is both an affront to easy-believism and a spotlight on the promises of God's Word. A comforting wake-up call."

—Dr. Ed Stetzer, president, Lifeway Research

"This is a book I wish was available when I turned twenty and had a terrible season of doubting my salvation. By God's grace and the truth of the gospel I was able to settle the issue. I have lived in the full assurance of my salvation in Jesus ever since. God wants us to experience the joyful truth that we are eternally secure in Jesus. This book can help take you there. I will be recommending this book often!"

—Dr. Daniel L. Akin, president,
Southeastern Baptist Theological Seminary

"As someone who works with young people, I often see the pitfall that my friend J.D. Greear explores in *Stop Asking Jesus Into Your Heart*; How To Know for Sure You are Saved. I have sat with many eighteen to twenty-four year olds that say they had no clue what they were doing when they repeated a prayer with someone as a young person. As next generation leaders, we have to focus on true life-change, really direction change rather than just a spiritual transaction. I am thankful that J.D. was willing to take on the hard discussions related to salvation and discipleship in this new book."

—J. Roger Davis, president, Student Life

"*Stop Asking Jesus Into Your Heart* by J.D. Greear is a biblical clarification for the assurance of salvation to the Christian based upon the finished work of Jesus Christ. The invitation to eternal life is more than a prayer! It is a living, breathing, real, relevant, relationship with God through Jesus Christ while being sealed by the Holy Spirit. The gospel saves and sustains! Read, reflect, and rejoice in the ability to know of the assurance of your salvation!

—Ed Newton, Bible Communicator, Memphis, TN

"When I first read the title, I was caught off guard—because I am an evangelist who continually urges hearers to repent and ask Jesus into their heart. Once I began to read, however, I began to understand the big idea—praying a prayer of repentance and salvation ought only to mark the beginning of a lifetime of repentance and faith. J.D. wrestles with a tough subject here and does a tremendous job of helping the church come to grips with a salvation not anchored in a one-time prayer but the finished work of Christ."

—Clayton King, teaching pastor, NewSpring Church,
and campus pastor, Liberty University

"This book is similar to John Stott's *Basic Christianity* in that it lays out with clarity and reasoned arguments the path to Christian belief. *Stop Asking Jesus Into Your Heart* is especially helpful in answering many follow-on questions, too. Faith seekers and faith sharers alike will benefit from J.D. Greear's clear thinking on what effectuates and evidences true salvation in Christ."

—David A. Spence, An Executor of Dr. Stott's Literary Estate

"Improper methodology and sloppy theology have paralyzed at worst and confused at best many of our churches today when it comes to evangelism. J.D.'s book is not only timely but crucial."

—Mike Calhoun, executive assistant to the president,
Word of Life Fellowship, Inc., and
author of *Where Was God When: Real Answers to Hard Questions*

"J.D. tackles an incredibly vital topic in our time, but from the front lines of ministry as one who stands unashamed to call people to follow Christ. Read this book and understand with fresh eyes and a hungry heart the wonder of biblical conversion."

—Dr. Alvin Reid, Professor of Evangelism & Student Ministry/ Bailey Smith Chair of Evangelism, Southeastern Baptist Theological Seminary and author of *As You Go: Creating a Gospel-Centered Culture of Missional Students*

"I wore out 2 Sharpies worth of ink writing 'Amen & WOW' in the margins of this new book. Chapter after chapter I was encouraged, rebuked, discipled, and compelled to be a better minister of the gospel. Thank you J.D. for this gift to the church."

—David Nasser, pastor/author/evangelist

"I have to admit the title of this book made me uncomfortable. It sounded to me like a tract against the so-called 'sinner's prayer,' and I find it biblical to cry out 'Lord have mercy on me, a sinner!' But as I read this book I found that is not what it is about at all. In this volume, J. D. Greear, one of the most dynamic and brilliant pastors in evangelical life today, addresses a common problem among Christians: the sense that we can never get assured enough that Jesus hears our sinners prayer and receives us, just as we are. This book throws the spotlight on Jesus as a welcoming, merciful Savior who joyously receives all who come to Him. This book could help free you, or someone you love, from the nagging fear that Jesus is trying to keep you out of His kingdom."

—Dr. Russell D. Moore, dean, Southern Baptist Theological Seminary, and author of *Tempted and Tried: Temptation and Triumph of Christ*

STOP ASKING JESUS INTO YOUR HE♥RT

HOW TO KNOW FOR SURE YOU ARE SAVED

J.D. GREEAR

PUBLISHING GROUP
NASHVILLE, TENNESSEE

978-1-4336-7921-6

Published by B&H Publishing Group
Nashville, Tennessee

Dewey: 234
Subject Heading: SALVATION \ FAITH \ ASSURANCE (THEOLOGY)

3 4 5 6 7 8 9 • 17 16 15 14 13

DEDICATION

To my parents, Lynn and Carol Greear, who taught me the importance of first fleeing to Christ and then of resting in Christ.

To my first pastor, Dr. E. C. Sheehan, who modeled for me the power of the gospel and acquainted me with those great spiritual pilgrims of the past who had embarked on this journey before me.

To my four children, Kharis, Alethia, Ryah, and Adon: May you find the joy of knowing the steadfast love of Christ as the anchor for your soul.

ACKNOWLEDGMENTS

I want to say a special thanks to Jedidiah Coppenger and his very capable team at B&H for devoting such energy to getting this book together. Their passion for their work makes it clear they see their work not just as a business, but as a ministry.

CONTENTS

FOREWORD

As recently as this week, I encountered a wonderful young man who has been desperately concerned about the state of his soul. Although for one man to see or know the heart of another is impossible, I felt certain that he knew the Lord. His angst over failures subsequent to his experience with Christ seemed to me to be more related to the family situation from which he came and the extent of the use of foreign substances in his life than it did to any substantive reason to doubt his salvation.

This book, *Stop Asking Jesus Into Your Heart,* is the book I needed to place in his hands. I fully believe that its message is perfectly designed to meet the needs of that young man and hundreds of others just like him. I confess that I dislike the title of the book, but J.D. Greear makes it clear that he has no objection to anyone receiving the Lord since the Bible clearly says, "To them that receive Him, to them gave He the authority to become the sons of God." In fact, while I might disagree with some interpretations here or there, I found this book thoroughly biblical. The title itself is not meant to prevent anyone from calling on the Lord. It is rather a genuine admonition for everyone to seek and trust the Lord Jesus.

However, not only is the book a biblical work, it is also a profound reflection of the nature of salvation. Salvation is the most complicated subject in Holy Scripture. The longer I study it, the more convinced I am that no one has a total grasp of its meaning since in the end it is an act of God that we cannot fully fathom. But for all of its difficulties, salvation is also wonderfully simple. Salvation is simple in terms of how people obtain it. Part of the mystery at work is that God took the complex notion of salvation and in His genius made it understandable enough for any man or woman to grasp. This short book demonstrates just how true that is.

J.D. operates with the training of a theologian but the heart of a pastor. In addition to his own experience, J.D. spends untold hours among his people. He loves them, feels their hurts and needs, and has learned to respond in a pastoral way. This book will be interesting for theologians but remains totally readable for the average church member. And perhaps most important of all, the seeker whose heart God is opening will be able to read this book, comprehend its message, and place his faith in Christ. Finally, it never hurts anyone to be called to a higher standard. This small volume challenges you to be sure that you are discussing critical theological issues in the clearest possible biblical terms and that you resist the temptation to think of such concepts in the more popular ways that are often in vogue. So take this book by Greear, read its message closely, profit by it as I have, and then pass it along to someone struggling with the question of whether or not he has been saved. If he has not, the book tells him how to gain salvation. If he has been saved, the book's message will confirm that to him in every way.

Paige Patterson, President
Southwestern Baptist Theological Seminary
Fort Worth, Texas

BAPTIZED
FOUR TIMES

If there were a *Guinness Book of World Records* record for "amount of times having asked Jesus into your heart," I'm pretty sure I would hold it.

By the time I reached the age of eighteen I had probably "asked Jesus into my heart" five thousand times. I started somewhere around age four when I approached my parents one Saturday morning asking how someone could know that they were going to heaven. They carefully led me down the "Romans Road to Salvation," and I gave Jesus His first invitation into my heart.

Both my parents and my pastor felt confident of my sincerity and my grasp on the details, and so I was baptized. We wrote the date in my Bible and I lived in peace about the matter for nearly a decade.

One Friday night during my ninth grade year, however, my Sunday school teacher told us that according to Matthew 7:21–23 many people who think they know Jesus will awaken on that final day to the reality that He never really knew them. Though they had prayed a prayer to receive Jesus, they had never really been born again and never taken the lordship of Jesus seriously. They would, my teacher explained, be turned away from heaven into everlasting punishment with the disastrous words, "I never knew you; depart from Me, you who practice lawlessness!"

I was terrified. Would I be one of those ones turned away? Had I really been "sorry" for my sins at age five? And could I *really* have known what I was doing *at age four*?

So I asked Jesus to come into my heart again, this time with a resolve to be much more intentional about my faith. I requested re-baptism, and gave a very moving testimony in front of our congregation about getting serious with God.

Case closed, right? Wrong.

> *I walked a lot of aisles during those days. I think I've been saved at least once in every denomination.*

Not long after that I found myself asking again: Had I *really* been sorry enough for my sin this time around? I'd see some people weep rivers of tears when they got saved, but I hadn't. Did that mean I was not really sorry? And there were a few sins I seemed to fall back into over and over again, no matter how many resolutions I made to do better. Was I *really* sorry for those sins? Was that prayer a moment of total surrender? Would I have died for Jesus at that moment if He'd asked?

So I prayed the sinner's prayer again. And again. And again. Each time trying to get it right, each time really trying to mean it. I would have a moment when I felt like I got it right, followed by a temporary euphoria. But it would fade quickly and I'd question it all again. And so I'd pray again.

I walked a lot of aisles during those days. I think I've been saved at least once in every denomination.

Because I understood baptism to be a post-salvation confession of faith, each time I gained a little assurance, I felt like I should get re-baptized. Four times, total. Honestly, it got pretty embarrassing. I became a staple at our church's baptism services. I got my own locker in the baptismal changing area.

It was a wretched experience. My spiritual life was characterized by cycles of doubt, aisle-walking, and submersion in water. I could not find the assurance of salvation no matter how often, or how sincerely, I asked Jesus into my heart.

I used to think I was alone in this struggle, but as I've shared my story over the years so many have come forward to tell me that my experience was theirs (usually minus the baptisms and the OCD tendencies) that I've concluded this problem is epidemic in the church.

Maybe that's why you've picked up this book. Maybe, despite your repeated sinner's prayers, you're still wondering if God will, in the end, open up the gates of heaven to you. You hope that He will, but enough doubt lingers to rob you of that elusive peace others seem to have.

Or maybe you have no idea whether you're going to heaven, and you are curious as to how anyone could possibly know something like that. Or maybe you wonder whether somebody who sins as much as you could ever be forgiven. Maybe you fear that you've said "no" to God so many times that you've forfeited any chance of salvation.

This book is written for all those groups, because they are all asking the same, simple question: *How can anyone know, beyond all doubt, that they are saved?*

The Other Side of the Problem: The Falsely Assured

This is a very serious question, not just because it keeps some people in a state of fear, but because others are getting it dead wrong.

Jesus warned that there are a vast number of people who seem assured of a salvation they don't actually possess. My Sunday school teacher was telling us the truth: according to Matthew 7, Jesus will turn away "many" on that last day who thought they belonged to Him. There's no doubt that many of those will have prayed a sinner's prayer.

One afternoon I was at a local basketball court and started a pickup game with a guy I'd seen there a few times. He was quite a character—he cursed like a sailor and had so many tattoos on his body I wasn't sure what the actual color of his skin was. He boasted continually about how many girls he was sleeping with. He wasn't the kind of guy you'd suspect knew his way around the Bible.

As we played our game, I began to share my story of how I came to Christ. About three sentences into it, he stopped, grabbed the ball, and said, "Dude, are you trying to *witness* to me?"

Surprised he even knew the term *witness*, I said, "Uhhh . . . well . . . yes."

He said, "That's awesome. No one has tried to witness to me in a long time. . . . But don't worry about me. I went to youth camp when I was thirteen and I asked Jesus to come into my heart. And I was legit. I became a super-Christian. I went to youth group every week, I did the "true love waits" commitment thing, I memorized verses, and went on mission trips. I even led other friends to Jesus.

"About two years after that, however, I 'discovered' *sex*. And I didn't like the idea of a god telling me who I could have sex with. So I decided to put God on hold for a while, and after a while just quit believing in Him altogether. I'm a happy atheist now."

He then added: "But here's what's awesome: the church I grew up in was Southern Baptist, and they taught eternal security—that means 'once saved, always saved.' By the way, aren't you a Baptist?"

****awkward silence from me****

He went on, "That means that my salvation at age thirteen still holds, even if I don't believe in God anymore now. 'Once saved, always saved,' right? That means that even if you're right, and God exists and Jesus is the only way, I'm safe! So either way, works out great for me. . . . If I'm right, then I haven't wasted my life curbing my lifestyle because of a fairy tale. OK, it's your shot."

What do you say to a person like that? Consider the facts: He had indeed prayed to ask Jesus into his heart, and all indications were that he was very sincere. And it's very possible for people to come to faith very early in life—Jesus, in fact, told adults to become like children if they want to be saved! Furthermore, this guy showed immediate "fruit" after his conversion, getting excited about Jesus and being busy for Him. And the Bible does indeed teach eternal security—once saved, always saved. So was he right? Can he, because he made a decision at some point in the past, live with the assurance that he is saved forever, regardless of how he lives now?

Here's the short answer, one I'll spend the rest of the book unpacking: *he cannot*. Salvation does indeed happen in a moment, and once you are saved you are always saved. The mark, however, of someone who is saved is that they maintain their confession of faith until the end of their lives. Salvation is not a prayer you pray in a one-time ceremony and then move on from; salvation is a posture of repentance and faith that you begin in a moment and maintain for the rest of your life.

> *Salvation is a posture of repentance and faith that you begin in a moment and maintain for the rest of your life.*

In His parable about the different types of soil, Jesus spoke of a group who heard His word and made an initial, encouraging response of belief, only to fade away over time. These are those, Jesus explained, who hear the gospel and respond positively to it—i.e., pray the prayer, walk the aisle, get baptized, or do whatever new converts in your church do. They remain in the church for a period of time. But they do not endure when the sun of persecution comes out and will not in the end be saved (Luke 8:13).

The apostle John described a large group of people who "believed in His name" but to whom Jesus would not commit Himself because "He knew all men" (John 2:23–25). He knew their belief was a temporary fad that would not endure the test of time and trial.

These sobering stories teach us that many are headed into eternal judgment under the delusion of going to heaven. They were told that if they prayed the prayer, Jesus would save them, seal them, and never leave nor forsake them. They prayed that prayer and lived under the delusion they will go to heaven when they die. My blood runs cold just thinking about them.

A 2011 Barna study[1] shows that nearly half of all adults in America have prayed such a prayer, and subsequently believe they are going to heaven, though many of them rarely, if ever, attend a church, read the Bible personally, or have lifestyles that differ in any significant way from those outside the church. If the groups described in Matthew 7 and Luke 8 are not referring to them, I don't know to whom they could be referring.

The Enemy—one of whose names in Scripture is "the Deceiver"—loves to keep truly saved believers unsure of their salvation because he knows that if he does they'll never experience the freedom, joy, and confidence that God wants them to have. But he also loves to keep those on their way to hell deluded into thinking they are on their way to heaven, their consciences immunized from Jesus' pleas to repent.

An Unhelpful Gospel Cliché?

I have begun to wonder if both problems, needless doubting and false assurance, are exacerbated by the clichéd ways in which we (as evangelicals) speak about the gospel. Evangelical shorthand for the gospel is to "ask Jesus into your heart," or "accept Jesus as Lord and Savior," or "give your heart to Jesus." These phrases may not be wrong in themselves, but the Bible never tells us, specifically, to seek salvation in those ways. The biblical summation of a saving response toward Christ is "repentance" and "belief" in the gospel.

"Belief," as I'll explain later, means acknowledging that God told the truth about Jesus, namely that He is Lord and that He has finished forever the work of our salvation.

> "He who believes in the Son has everlasting life; and he who does not believe the Son shall not see life, but the wrath of God abides on him." (John 3:36)

> "Sirs, what must I do to be saved?" . . . "Believe on the Lord Jesus, and you will be saved." (Acts 16:30–31 HCSB)

> To him who does not work but believes on Him who justifies the ungodly, his faith is accounted for righteousness. (Rom. 4:5)

> If you confess with your mouth the Lord Jesus and believe in your heart that God has raised Him from the dead, you will be saved. For with the heart one believes unto righteousness, and with the mouth confession is made unto salvation. (Rom. 10:9–10)

Repentance (which we'll also get into more deeply later) means "acting" on that belief. Repentance means reversing your direction based on who you understand Jesus to be. It was the first response Jesus called for in His preaching of the gospel (Mark 1:15), and what Paul said God had commanded all men everywhere to do now that Jesus had been resurrected (Acts 17:30). Apart from repentance there is no salvation.

You can "ask Jesus into your heart" without repenting and believing, and you can repent and believe without articulating a request for Jesus to come into your heart.

Repentance and faith are heart postures you take toward the finished work of Christ. You might express the beginning of that posture in a prayer. But don't make the mistake of equating that prayer with the posture. The sinner's prayer is not a magic incantation or a recipe you follow to get a salvation cake. The real stuff—the stuff that matters—is the posture of repentance and faith behind the words you speak. The prayer is good only insofar as it verbalizes the posture.

Placing an overemphasis on phrases like "ask Jesus into your heart" gives assurance to some who shouldn't have it and keeps it from some who should.

Clarifying Two Things I Am Not Saying

I'm Not Saying "Asking Jesus into Your Heart Is Heretical"

When we are "saved," Jesus does indeed "come into our hearts," at least in a manner of speaking (see, for example, Rom. 8:9–11; Eph. 3:17; Col. 1:27–28; Gal. 2:20). But there are lots of other things that happen at the moment of salvation, too: we are washed in Jesus' blood, sealed by His Spirit, guaranteed a dwelling place in the new heaven, grafted into the vine, have our names written in the Lamb's Book of Life, Satan's claims against us are nullified, etc. *Asking Jesus to do any one of these for us at the moment of salvation is not heretical, but by focusing on any one of them we run the risk of obscuring the one thing necessary for salvation—a posture of repentance toward and faith in His finished work (Mark 1:15; John 3:36; Rom. 4:5; 10:9–10).*

For example, if we go around telling people that if they want to be saved they should ask Jesus to "begin construction on my home in heaven" (John 14:1–3), or "put my name in the Lamb's Book of Life" (Rev. 21:27), that would not be wrong, per se, but it could be misleading. People with no remorse for their sin might still be excited about Jesus providing them with an eternal vacation home or getting their name onto some heavenly honor-roll list.

That said, "asking Jesus into your heart" is among the more biblical summations of salvation, if the concepts behind the words are understood. "Heart" in the Bible (Prov. 4:23) is the seat of the person. Having Jesus come into your heart, in that sense, would mean that He fuses Himself into the deepest part of who you are—that you rest your hopes upon His righteousness, lean on Him for strength, and submit to His Lordship at your core. God fusing Himself to the believer at salvation is what the church fathers called *theosis* (translated *divinization*), whereby Christ literally unites His Spirit with ours (1 Cor. 12:13; Gal. 2:20). Christ is, in that sense, "in our hearts."

> *"Praying the sinner's prayer" has become something like a Protestant ritual we have people go through to gain entry into heaven.*

Ultimately, my concern is not on what words or actions we might use to express our faith in Christ but that we don't substitute those words or actions for repentance and faith. "Praying the sinner's prayer" has become something like a Protestant ritual we have people go through to gain entry into heaven. As "gospel shorthand," it presents salvation as a transaction one conducts with Jesus and moves on from rather than the beginning of a posture we take toward the finished work of Christ and maintain for the rest of our lives.

I'm Not Saying We Should Hesitate Pressing for a Decision When We Present the Gospel

Preachers in the revivalist traditions called for sinners to respond immediately to the gospel by walking an aisle or asking Jesus into your heart. While this may not be my preferred technique, the gospel is indeed an invitation and each time it is preached that invitation ought to be extended in some form (e.g., John 1:12; Matt. 11:28; Rev. 22:17). In fact, if we do not urge the hearer to respond personally to God's offer in Christ, I do not believe we have fully preached the gospel.

> *If we do not urge the hearer to respond personally to God's offer in Christ, I do not believe we have fully preached the gospel.*

Calling on sinners to seek salvation on the spot is not something invented by the Finney-Revivalist tradition. Throughout history, even some of the most Reformed evangelists have invited hearers to pray a sinner's prayer.

For example, Charles Spurgeon ended one of his sermons by saying,

> Before you leave this place, breathe an earnest prayer to God, saying, "God be merciful to me a sinner. Lord, I need to be saved. Save me. I call upon thy name." Join with me in prayer at this moment, I entreat you. Join with me while I put words into your mouths, and speak them on your behalf—"Lord, I am guilty. I deserve thy wrath. Lord, I cannot save myself. . . . I cast myself wholly upon thee, O Lord. I trust the

blood and righteousness of thy dear Son; I trust thy mercy, and thy love, and thy power, as they are revealed in him. I dare to lay hold upon this word of thine, that whosoever shall call on the name of the Lord shall be saved. Lord, save me tonight, for Jesus' sake. Amen."[2]

George Whitefield extended the same kind of invitations.[3] John Bunyan described one of his characters, "Hopeful," being led through a sinner's prayer by another, "Faithful."[4] The apostle Peter invited three thousand people to come forward for baptism in response to his first sermon (Acts 2:38). Ananias led Paul to call on God's name for forgiveness of sins after their first conversation (Acts 22:16).

So I am not, in any way, trying to discourage calling for a decision when we present the gospel. I am saying that above all else we must emphasize the absolute indispensability of repentance and faith for salvation.

> *Salvation is not given because you prayed a prayer correctly, but because you have leaned the hopes of your soul on the finished work of Christ.*

I am also saying to those who, like me, have asked Jesus into their hearts thousands of times, that they can "stop asking Jesus into their heart" and start resting in the finished work of Christ. Salvation comes not because you prayed a prayer correctly, but because you have leaned the hopes of your soul on the finished work of Christ.

Shorthand phrases for the gospel can serve a good purpose, insofar as everyone knows exactly what they mean. But in light of the fact that so many in our country seem assured of a salvation they give no evidence of having because of a prayer they prayed, and so many others are unable to find assurance no matter how often they pray that prayer, I believe it is time to put the shorthand aside and preach simply salvation by repentance toward God and faith in the finished work of Christ. Or, at least, to be careful to explain exactly what we mean when we call for a response to the gospel.

The Path Ahead

Here's where we'll go from here. First, I will show you why assurance is so important and how we know God wants us to possess it. Then we will look at the core of the gospel message, Christ's substitutionary work on our behalf. After that we will take a close look at what the Bible means by words like *belief* and *repentance*. Then we'll try to understand why if "once saved, always saved," the Bible always seems to be warning us that we can lose our salvation. After that we'll consider what the Bible tells us are the evidences that we have really believed, and finally, we'll consider what we should do if we continue to doubt.

My prayer is that by the time we're done, you'll know exactly where you stand with God. I hope to show you how to base your assurance on a promise God gave once for all in Christ and not on the fleeting memory of a prayer you once prayed.

Perhaps you are reading this and already realize that the words you once prayed to God were not accompanied by genuine repentance and faith. Like millions of "Christians," you prayed a prayer, but you have yet to submit to Him as Lord of your life. I would encourage you to settle that now, before we begin this journey. If you are ready to take Jesus seriously, He is ready to share with you the joy He has prepared for you from all eternity (Jer. 29:13).

DOES GOD EVEN WANT US TO HAVE ASSURANCE?

Does God really want us to have assurance of our salvation?

I've heard people argue that He does not. They suppose that this kind of assurance is presumptuous on our part, if not downright arrogant. Furthermore, wouldn't God get more out of us by holding the *possibility* of salvation over our heads, the way an employer might motivate their staff with the threat of layoffs or offer of bonuses?

I can say with certainty that God wants you to have certainty about your salvation. He changes, encourages, and motivates us not by the uncertainty of fear, but by the security of love. That is one of the things that makes the gospel absolutely distinct from all other religious messages in the world.

In fact, I'll be so bold as to say that your spiritual life will *really* never take off until you have the assurance of salvation. Until you know that you are His and He is yours, your obedience will be limited. Your love will be stifled, your confidence will be shaky, and your courage will be minimal.

It is only through assurance of love that we find the strength to endure all manner of opposition, doubt, and trial.

How can you stand against a hostile world if you are not assured of the God whom you are leaving it all for? How can you take up the cross if you're not convinced of your resurrection? Can you really "jump" with abandon into the darkness if you're not convinced that Someone is actually going to catch you? It is the joy of knowing beyond doubt that you belong to God that makes all of these things possible.

> *How can you take up the cross if you're not convinced of your resurrection?*

Reckless Obedience

It is extremely difficult to risk it all for something when you're not convinced the something you are risking it all for actually exists. When I was in high school I took up rock climbing as a hobby. One day a friend suggested that instead of climbing up the rock face, we repel down it. I'd never done that before, but he claimed he was an expert. Because I was an idiot, I believed him.

There were four of us on the mountain that day. Somehow I got volunteered to go first. (The fact that my "expert" friend did not volunteer to be first should have been a signal to me that something was amiss.) We tied my belay rope around a tree, and I stood with my back toward a 75-foot drop. My friend told me to "lean back." If you've never done this before, let me summarize my thoughts at that moment:

PANIC.

Lean back? Intentionally lean backward toward certain death, held only by a rope secured to a tree by a friend whose mouth consistently wrote checks his brain couldn't cash? (My perspective on life and character and friendship matured significantly in the space of those few seconds.) But though I may have suddenly gotten wiser in that moment, my manhood was also on the line. (When you're sixteen, your manhood is always on the line.) My friends stood waiting to ridicule. This was the moment of truth. Men are made in these moments. (For the record, so are martyrs.)

I stood there for a few seconds working up my courage. I prayed to receive Jesus into my heart one more time (not kidding). I crossed myself just in case the Catholics are right after all (kidding). And then I leaned back. Fully committed. All-in.

What was surely no longer than a nanosecond seemed like an eternity as I waited for the rope to catch me. When it did, I stood, perpendicular to the rock face and parallel to the ground, suspended in the air by a rope and a flimsy tree. My friend said, "Now jump backwards." Once again calling forth every ounce of courage I could muster, I leapt off of the rock with all my might. I sprung about 2 inches. Another jump—6 inches. Another—4 feet. Then 10 feet. A few jumps later, I was standing on terra firma. I'm pretty sure at that point I spoke in tongues.

My high school best friend was next. He'd never done it before either. Now, let me explain something about this guy: he was better looking than I was, more athletic, more popular, and better with the ladies. I hated that kid, but he was my "best friend." He was also, to note, scared of heights. From seventy-five feet below I could hear him being given the instructions. But when it came time to lean back, he didn't budge. That is, if you don't count shaking in terror. After about ten minutes he finally took one of his legs and felt down below for a foothold. He found one, and then another and then another. He slowly worked his way down the rock face, one foothold at a time.

Of course, that's not repelling. That is rock climbing with repelling equipment.

My friend came to a place where the rock face took a significant turn inward, meaning that there was no longer any way to get a foothold. To get over this spot he'd have to let go of the rock altogether and lean back on the rope.

He hesitated. He considered. He prayed. He climbed back up.

He had gotten to a place on the rock that could only be passed by leaning your full weight on the rope. Because he did not have confidence in his rope, he could not make it past that point.

In the same way, there are points you can never pass spiritually until you are confident that Jesus will support the full weight of your soul. There are sacrifices you'll never make and commands you'll never obey unless you are convinced of their eternal value.

> *In the same way, there are points you can never pass spiritually until you are confident that Jesus will support the full weight of your soul.*

Following Jesus, after all, means saying "no" to a lot of things. To take up the cross means delivering yourself over to death. Death of control over your life. Death of your own dreams. The release of everything you have to Him. That death is empowered only by the assurance of new life.[1]

You'll never have the courage to embrace the cross until you have the confidence that you own the resurrection.

You will never have the strength to say "no" to sin until you realize the unconditional "yes" that God has given to you in Christ.

You'll never give up your life in radical obedience until you are radically assured of His radical commitment to you.

One of the reasons Paul was unmoved by suffering and persecution was that he was certain of where he stood with God. "For this reason I also suffer these things," he said, "for I know whom I have believed and am persuaded that He is able to keep what I have committed to Him until that Day" (2 Tim. 1:12).

> *You'll never give up your life in radical obedience until you are radically assured of His radical commitment to you.*

Furthermore, when you're not assured of God's love for you, your motivations for obedience will become corrupted. You'll do good works in the hopes that God will approve of you because of them. This is not really love for God; it's self-preservation. Only the security of knowing God has accepted you can free you to seek God for His own sake. Apart from that assurance, you can fear God like a slave master, but you'll never love Him like a father. That's what true obedience is—beyond merely adhering to a set of regulations; it is doing so because you deeply and truly love the One commanding you.

Religion commands us to change our behavior, but it cannot change our hearts. It can tell us to do what is right, but cannot give us a love for the right. Only the gospel and the assurance it yields creates a passion for the right in our hearts, because only the gospel goes deep enough to actually change the warped nature of our hearts. The apostle Paul said that it is only as we are overwhelmed at the glory of Christ's sacrifice for us that

> *Religion commands us to change our behavior, but it cannot change our hearts.*

we are *transformed* into glory ourselves—the glory of people who serve God because they crave God and who do righteousness because they love righteousness. The fruits of the Spirit, he said—things like love, joy, peace, patience, and kindness—grow only in the soul of the assurance of God's love for us.[2]

So, far from killing our motivation for obedience or spiritual growth, assurance *fuels* it. Only confidence in God's commitment to you will inspire confidence in your commitment to Him. Only joy in what you know you possess in Him will enable you to leave everything else behind. Only knowing the love of God for you produces love for God in you.

Children, Spouses, and Friends

Jesus knew how important it was for His disciples to be assured of His love. In the final conversation He had with them before He died, He used three metaphors that showed them how committed He was to them. They were about to go through hell on earth, and He wanted to give them something to hang onto that would sustain them in that hour of great tribulation.[3]

His Beloved Children

In John 14:18, Jesus said, "I will not leave you orphans; I will come to you."

A faithful father does not leave his kids wondering whether or not he loves them. When I have to go away on a trip, I don't say to my kids, "Daddy will be back soon . . . or maybe he won't. Maybe I'm not really your daddy at all. Maybe my real family lives somewhere else. You'll just have to wait and see if I come back. Sit around and think about that while I'm gone, and let that compel you to become better children."

That would not produce love and loyalty in my children. It might produce a little fear-based obedience, but it's only a matter of time until fear-based obedience turns into father-loathing rebellion. If I don't want my own children fearing they might be orphans, would God?

Do we really think we are better fathers to our children than God would be to His? Hardly. The love God has for us is the highest in the universe. Jesus said, "As the Father loved Me, I also have loved you" (John 15:9). Jesus loves us like God the Father loved Him, and He wants us to have the same assurance with Him that He had with God.

Think about that. The same love the perfect Father has for the perfect Son is the love that Christ, our everlasting Father, now has for us.[4] I have a hard time really getting my mind around that. But if the Son of God doesn't sit around wondering about His relationship to His Father, I should not be worried about my relationship to Him. When you become a Christian you are actually placed in Christ and Christ into you, and just as Christ could never be cast out from the Father, neither can you.[5] That is assurance if there ever was such a thing.

His Betrothed

In that same conversation Jesus told His disciples,

> "Let not your heart be troubled; you believe in God,
> believe also in Me. In My Father's house are many mansions;
> if it were not so, I would have told you. I go to prepare a place
> for you. And if I go and prepare a place for you, I will come
> again and receive you to Myself; that where I am, there you
> may be also." (John 14:1–3)

Some have noted that Jesus' language in these verses is laden with Jewish wedding imagery. In Jesus' day, a young suitor would travel to his beloved's home, throw a party, and request her hand in marriage.

Assuming she said yes, he would return to his father's home where he would begin construction on a room attached to the family living space. When their "place" was completed, he would return for her. Before he left, he would promise her that he was coming back.[6]

He did not want her to worry. Worry might lead to doubt, and doubt would cause her to be open to the advances of other suitors. He wanted her assurance to be so strong that she would not be moved by the flirtations of another.

When my wife and I got engaged, she was a student at the University of Virginia and I was attending a seminary in North Carolina. The hardest thing for us to do was to say good-bye each weekend and return to our respective homes to endure another week of classes apart. The last thing I would have wanted was for her to wonder if I really loved her. If she doubted that, she might be open to the advances of other guys. So throughout our engagement I assured her repeatedly that nothing was going to stop me from marrying her. In fact, I gave her a big fat diamond to wear on her finger to prove it. She and I both knew that if I didn't come back for her, she was keeping that. So she spent her time in Virginia without any doubts about my commitment to her.

That assurance not only gave her peace, it gave her strength. She was not interested in the attention of other guys because of what she knew she had in me.

Jesus gave us, His beloved, that same confidence. He spoke to us in wedding language so we would have the confidence of the waiting bride. Only in that confidence are we able to resist the enticements of sin.

His Friends

Finally, in John 15:15 Jesus calls His disciples His "friends."

"No longer do I call you servants . . . but I have called you friends."

Do you want your best friends questioning your loyalty to them? One of the greatest aspects of friendship is the feeling of safety that comes with it. You can be yourself around them and say what's on your mind without worrying about them betraying your confidence or abandoning you. You can give them access to the most vulnerable parts of your life without any fear they will violate them. Until you get to that point it's not really a *friendship*, or at least not a very enjoyable one. True friendship only grows in security and trust.

I've had a few "friends" who broke my trust. I was never sure if they were guarding my reputation or trashing it. We didn't remain friends very long. The friends I have developed the deepest bonds with are those I know I could trust with my very life.

Jesus wants us no less sure of His friendship to us. He said,

"Greater love has no one than this, than to lay down one's life for his friends." (John 15:13)

His commitment to friendship is not less than ours; it is infinitely more! Perhaps you've had a friend betray you or discover something about you that led to their rejection of you. Jesus never will. From the beginning, He saw it all and chose us anyway (John 15:16). When we revealed our worst side to Jesus, He bore our shame and consequences in our place. Friendship doesn't get any more secure than that.

Those three images show us for certain that God wants us to be sure. He couldn't have chosen three more intimate and precious relationships! We are His children, His bride, and His friends.

During that same discussion He told us to abide in that assurance,[7] because only as we abide in Him—that is, *rest* in that assurance—will the fruits of righteousness grow in us.

The Damnable Doctrine of Doubt

Every religious message except for the gospel uses doubt and uncertainty to compel obedience. But God is not simply after obedience; He's after *a whole new kind of obedience,* the obedience that grows from desire.[8] An obedience that obeys because it wants to, not just because it has to.

The established Church of Martin Luther's day believed that people would only obey when they were threatened with harsh consequences for rebellion. Luther decried this as the *"damnable doctrine of doubt."*[9] Being afraid of judgment will indeed produce a surface-level adherence to the law, he said, but beneath that thin veneer of obedience will rush a river of fear, pride, and self-interest. The only way to develop real love for God is to have fear removed. As the apostle John said, God's great love for us is what produces love for God in us.[10]

Similarly, the seventeenth-century leaders of the established Church in England placed John Bunyan, the author of *Pilgrim's Progress*, in prison for preaching the gospel of God's unmerited grace toward sinners. Their argument was that when the fear of punishment is removed, people would run wild, doing whatever they wanted. Bunyan replied, "If people really see that Christ has removed the fear of punishment from them by taking it into Himself, they won't do whatever they want, they'll do whatever *He* wants."[11]

The gospel of God's grace creates in us the *desire* to obey. My four kids (who are currently all under the age of ten) know that I miss them terribly when I am gone on a trip. So when I return, they rush outside to my car the moment they hear the garage door open, pile in through the driver's door, climb onto my lap, and say, "Daddy, what did you get for us on your trip?"

When they think I am mad at them, or that I'm in a bad mood, however, they tend to avoid me, preferring to play in rooms where I'm not present. They might obey my instructions to the letter, but they don't want to be close to me.

> *God wants the intimacy of sons, not just the service of slaves.*

It works the same with God. Knowing He cherishes us makes us want to draw close; fear makes us withdraw, even if we are obeying His commandments. God wants the intimacy of sons, not just the service of slaves.

How Can We Find the Assurance of a Child, a Bride, and a Friend?

Despite God's intent for us to possess the assurance of a treasured child, a beloved bride, and a cherished friend, it still seems to allude some of us.

That's probably why in his first letter to the church, the apostle John explored how believers can know—*know*—that they have eternal life. (This must have been a really important issue to John. He recorded the three metaphors we looked at above and made assurance the subject of his first letter to the church.) He ended that letter by saying:

> These things I have written to you who believe in the name of the Son of God, that you may know that you have eternal life. (1 John 5:13)

Know. Not "hope." Not "be reasonably sure." *Know.* And how does he say we know?

> He who believes in the Son of God has the witness in himself; he who does not believe God has made Him a liar, because he has not believed the testimony that God has given of his Son. And this is the testimony: that God has given us eternal life, and this life is in His Son. He who has the Son has

life; he who does not have the Son of God does not have life.
(1 John 5:10–12)

In these verses, John identified two components of assurance:

1.   *Belief in a testimony about eternal life.* John uses the word *believe* ninety times in the Gospel of John alone. He says that those who believe "have everlasting life."[12] Believing the testimony assures us we have eternal life.
2.   *Evidences of eternal life at work in us.* Eternal life is not just a reality we enter into when we die; it is something that comes into us now, and its evidences appear everywhere. Seeing those evidences assures us eternal life is in us.

We'll examine both of those components in the chapters that follow.

The assurance of a treasured child, a betrothed fiancée, and a cherished friend awaits us. So why not ask Jesus for the wisdom to understand what we're about to explore and the faith to enter into it?

3

JESUS IN MY PLACE

My first year of college was the worst year of my life, despite the fact that I had lots of friends, was in a good school, enjoying good grades, and looking forward to a reasonably bright future. The question of whether or not I was saved was driving me to despair. I had already been baptized twice but the issue of my salvation seemed no closer to being resolved.

I spent many a Friday night chained to my desk scouring obscure commentaries to figure out what various verses about repentance and faith really meant. I memorized large sections of the Bible. I did Greek word studies to determine subtle nuances or New Testament verses on the gospel. I prayed and fasted. I made vows. I talked with pastors, professors, and friends. I interviewed Charles Ryrie. I went out in the woods and yelled at God.

Why was He withholding assurance from me? Why was He hiding? Had He predestined me not to be saved, and was that why I couldn't find assurance? Or was He waiting on me to make some promise to Him—about going to the mission field or living in poverty or something—before He'd let me find assurance? Was He punishing me for my sin?

One day I got so angry at God that I asked Him why He didn't just make me a dog, since dogs at least don't have to worry about going to hell. Often, through tears, I pleaded with God that if He'd let me have an assurance of salvation, I'd be the best Christian who'd ever lived.

But no matter what I did, what promises I made, or how many times I asked Jesus into my heart, I could not shake the fear that I was headed for hell.

I could not shake the fear that I was headed for hell.

That might seem strange, almost delusional, to some people. But if you really believe in heaven and hell, how can you not be desperate to know which one you are headed to? Toward the end of that year, I began to conclude I could never really know. I wasn't sure what to do. I felt despair, like a dark storm cloud, coming over my heart.

My monkish behavior, however, got me the reputation for being a "serious" student of the Word. I was the guy too busy praying and studying the Bible to go out and have a good time. At the end of my freshman year I was approached by the director of Word of Life Christian camps, a large Christian student ministry in the Northeast, and asked to serve as one of his head counselors for the summer. I wanted to serve, but didn't see how someone who didn't know for sure if he was saved could be entrusted to look after the souls of others.

Mike patiently listened to me pour out my struggle to him. I told him I didn't think I could therefore do the job. He quietly opened his Bible to John 3:36 and asked me to read it aloud to him:

> "He who believes in the Son has everlasting life; and he
> who does not believe the Son shall not see life, but the wrath of
> God abides on him."

He said, "How many categories of people do you see in that verse?"

"Two," I answered.

"What are they?"

"Those who believe, and those who don't."

"Which are you, J.D.?"

Mike was showing me that there are only two postures we can take toward Jesus Christ. We either "believe" or we do not.[1] More literal translations of John 3:36 render the two categories of that verse "he who believes" and "he who does not obey."[2] The interchange of "believe" and "obey" is helpful—it shows us that belief and obedience are, in a way, synonyms. We are commanded to believe that Jesus did what He said He did: paid the full penalty of our sin and settled it forever, and then rearrange our life according to that belief. If we believe, we will obey. If we do not obey, we don't believe.

If John 3:36 is true, you are either, right now, in believing submission to Jesus Christ, or unbelieving rebellion. For all my time and energy, the answer was astoundingly simple: we either believe the Son, or we do not.

At the end of his first epistle, John says that whether or not we have eternal life is conditioned on whether we believe the "testimony" God has given about the work of Jesus. Again, there are only two options: believe it, or declare God a liar (1 John 5:10).

The Testimony

The "testimony" John refers to has several key components. John says,

> And this is the testimony: that God has given us eternal
> life, and this life is in His Son. (1 John 5:11)

The testimony is that eternal life is not something we have in ourselves, so God had to give it to us in Jesus. Believing the testimony thus first means admitting that there is no life in us, and no potential to change that on our own, John says,

> If we say that we have no sin, we deceive ourselves, and the truth [read: the testimony] is not in us. . . . If we say that we have not sinned, we make Him a liar, and His word [read: the testimony] is not in us. (1 John 1:8, 10)

If we think that we have spiritual life in ourselves—that we are worthy of God's acceptance, or that we can be good enough to earn God's approval if we just try a little harder, or that God knows we are doing our best and will accept our good intentions—we reject God's testimony about the indispensability of Jesus and call Him a liar. The testimony is that we are hopelessly wicked, spiritually dead, and without hope apart from God's intervention.

Truly admitting unworthiness and inability is difficult because we have spent our whole lives trying to prove we are anything but *unworthy.*

Truly admitting unworthiness and inability is difficult because we have spent our whole lives trying to prove we are anything *but* unworthy. Most people will admit they make mistakes and are not perfect but far fewer will go on from there to admit their "mistakes" make them unworthy of eternal life and worthy of utter condemnation. We want to believe that our mistakes are not that bad, that deep down we are still pretty good people.

You can hear this in how we downplay the "badness" of our sin. We describe our sins as "mistakes," "lapses in judgment," or "indiscretions." We acknowledge we are not perfect, but maintain that, at our core, we are still good, decent people. Thus, we deserve *good* things—good salaries, respect, and recognition—and we'll fight anyone who challenges that.

If that's the case, God is a liar.

Believing the testimony means admitting that you are "unworthy" of any honor before God. Your sin really is *that* bad. God created you with the greatest position and privilege, and you spurned Him. You thought you'd be a better god to yourself than He would. You didn't start to sin because you hung around the wrong crowd; you were the wrong crowd. You hung around those you were comfortable with. You chose sin because you liked it better than God. No one taught you to sin; it came naturally. Like King David, you have been sinful from birth (Ps. 51:5). You deserve nothing but the wrath of God, with no qualifications and no exceptions.

Believing the testimony starts with admitting that there is no longer anything worthy of eternal life left in you. Thank God the testimony doesn't end there, but that's where it starts.

> [If we will acknowledge our sinfulness] . . . we have an
> Advocate with the Father, Jesus Christ the righteous. And He
> Himself is the propitiation for our sins, and not for ours only
> but also for the whole world. (1 John 2:1–2)

God has testified not only to our sinfulness, but also to His graciousness. He has told us that He so loved the world that He did for us what we could not do for ourselves. Jesus, God in the flesh, lived the life we should have lived and then died the death we had been condemned to die. By doing so He put away our death forever.

Advocate is a legal term, referring to someone who argues your case before the bar of justice on your behalf. The advocate God has given for our sin is "Jesus Christ the righteous."

Normally an advocate argues for your innocence—or, that you should not be punished based on extenuating circumstances, your general good character demonstrated in other places, etc. Our Advocate, John says, does no such thing. He never argues for our goodness. He argues His righteousness in our place.

The word *propitiation* means that a claim has been satisfied (literally, "wrath has been absorbed"). For example, if you caused a traffic accident, doing several thousand dollars' worth of damage to someone else's car, the account is not settled until you pay the damages. Only then is that person "propitiated." When the claim is paid in full, they have no more hold on you.

Jesus propitiated the holy wrath of God against our sin by suffering the full penalty for it in our place. Jesus does not argue our worthiness, He argues His substitution. We may not be worthy to be forgiven, but He is worthy to forgive us.

In 1 John 1:9, John says that Jesus is "*faithful* and *just* to forgive us our sins." Notice that John didn't say that God is "merciful" and "kind" to forgive our sins. That's because the basis of God's forgiveness of us is not mercy, it is justice. Jesus paid the full penalty for our sin; not an ounce of judgment remains. It would be unjust for God to hold the sins of Christians against them any longer, for He would be requiring two penalties for the same sin! If your spouse pays the power bill and the power company sends you the same bill and asks you to pay, you rightly protest that as unjust. In the same way, for God to exact one drop of punishment from the believer for

> *We may not be worthy to be forgiven, but He is worthy to forgive us.*

his sin would be requiring two penalties for the same sin. Jesus suffered the full extent of God's judgment; all that is left for me is acceptance.

When I had thought of Jesus standing before God begging for mercy, or leniency, on my behalf, it provided little comfort. I imagined Jesus going into the heavenly courtroom with a stack of case folders with one marked "Greear," which He pulled out and said, *"OK, Father, Greear again. Can you give him one more chance? He's a good kid, really. Please? Pretty please? Come on, Father, You owe Me. I went to earth and everything for You . . ."* Deep down I'd wonder when I would reach the end of God's patience—I'd sin for the 491st time and the Father would say, "That's it. No more leniency for Greear. Even with You in his corner, Jesus. He's going to have to pay for that one."[3]

> *Jesus suffered the full extent of God's judgment; all that is left for me is acceptance.*

Jesus, however, does not appeal to God for mercy on my behalf. He appeals for justice. He has satisfied all the claims against me, and now says to the Father, *"Father, I paid the full price for this sin. I took the penalty due to him so that he could have the credit due to Me. It is only right that he not be held accountable for that sin."*[4]

For those in Christ, this is the confidence we have before God. We don't *hope* we are forgiven, we *know* it, because our standing before God has nothing to do with our worthiness, but the worthiness of the Advocate who now stands in our place.

Most people hope that they are "good enough" to earn God's approval, to get on His "A-list." Comparatively speaking, they think, their sins have not been *that* bad. So as long as God grades on the curve they'll be fine. But this is direct defiance of "the testimony" God has given about Jesus. If we could have been "good enough," would Jesus really have had to die? What kind of God would have done that to Jesus if there were another way?[5]

Others try to buy forgiveness "on credit." They tell God that if He'll forgive them for their latest offense, they'll make it up to Him by some good work in the future. The testimony states that we could never be good enough to earn God's forgiveness. God doesn't forgive us on the basis of what we *will* do, but on the basis of what Jesus *has* done.[6]

Still others believe that when they die they will go to a "purgatory" where they can pay off the remaining balance of their sins. This also is a rejection of the testimony. Is Christ's work not completed, as He said it was?[7] Do we really complete His suffering by a little of our own?

We were so bad He had to die; He was so gracious He was glad to die.

There is one hope for sinners: the finished work of Christ. We do not need to add to it; we could not if we tried. "Believing the testimony" means embracing what God has said about the finished work of Christ on our behalf.

We were so bad He had to die for us; He was so gracious He was glad to die. When we repentantly believe that, we receive eternal life.

Jesus, Our High Priest

The Old Testament prophet Zechariah, writing five hundred years before Jesus was born on earth, gives us an incredible picture of the security Jesus' propitiatory work provides to us. Zechariah saw a vision of a high priest named Joshua about to enter the presence of God.

A little background: High priests offered a yearly sacrifice on "Yom Kippur" (literally, "the day of atonement"). They would enter the "Holy of Holies," the place in the Jewish temple where the presence of God dwelt. God's glory rested upon the top of ark of the covenant kept there, between the images of two cherubim mounted there. The Holy of Holies was separated from the rest of the temple by a thick veil, and could be entered only one time a year by the most high priest.

On "Yom Kippur," the high priest would go in, sprinkle the blood of a clean animal sacrifice upon the top of the ark, and thereby "propitiate" the anger of God against the sins of the people of Israel. The high priest was to make meticulous preparation to enter the Holy of Holies on that day, for he was coming into the very presence of God. If any defilement were found upon him, the book of Leviticus says, he would be struck down in God's presence. Some traditions say that small bells were placed on the edge of his robe and a rope tied around his ankle so that if he were struck down they could drag out his corpse without exposing themselves (though this last part might be a legend).[8]

Old Testament scholar Ray Dillard describes the intense process leading up to this moment:

> A week beforehand, the high priest was put into seclusion—taken away from his home and into a place where he was completely alone. Why? So he wouldn't accidentally touch or eat anything unclean. Clean food was brought to him, and he'd wash his body and prepare his heart. The night before the Day of Atonement he didn't go to bed; he stayed up all night praying and reading God's Word to purify his soul. Then on Yom Kippur he bathed head to toe and dressed in pure, unstained white linen. Then he went into the Holy of Holies and offered an animal sacrifice to God to atone, or pay the penalty for, his own sins. After that he came out and bathed completely again, and new white linen was put on him, and he went in again, this time sacrificing for the sins of the priests. But that's not all. He would come out a third time, and he bathed again from

head to toe and they dressed him in brand new pure linen, and
he went into the Holy of Holies and atoned for the sins of all
the people . . .

. . . this was all done in public. The temple was crowded,
and those in attendance watched closely. There was a thin
screen, and he bathed behind it. But the people were present:
They saw him bathe, dress, go in, come back out. He was their
representative before God, and they were there cheering him
on. They were very concerned to make sure that everything was
done properly and with purity, because he represented them
before God.[9]

To his horror, Zechariah sees Joshua, his high priest, about to enter
the Holy of Holies but covered in human excrement. This was disaster:
not only for Joshua; for all the people of Israel. This moment of represen-
tation by the high priest was their hope of forgiveness.

Just as Zechariah despairs, however, he hears the Lord speak:

"Take away the filthy garments from him." And to him
He said, "See, I have removed your iniquity from you, and I
will clothe you with rich robes. . . . And I will remove the iniquity of that land in one day." (Zech. 3:4, 9)

God had given Zechariah a vision of how we all, even the most
religious among us, look to God as we approach Him, and a promise
to remove that defilement from us forever "in a single day." Tim Keller
explains,

Centuries later another Joshua showed up, another Yeshua.
"Jesus," "Yeshua," "Joshua"—it's the same name in Aramaic,
Greek, and Hebrew. . . . He staged his own Day of Atonement.
One week beforehand, Jesus began to prepare. And the night
before, he didn't go to sleep—but what happened to Jesus was

exactly the reverse of what happened to Joshua the high priest, because instead of cheering him on, nearly everyone he loved betrayed, abandoned, or denied him. And when he stood before God, instead of receiving words of encouragement, the Father forsook him. Instead of being clothed in rich garments, he was stripped of the only garment he had, he was beaten, and he was killed naked. He was bathed . . . in human spit.[10]

Before God, we are like the filth-covered Yeshua that Zechariah saw. But because a new Yeshua, who was perfect, was clothed in our filth and suffered its consequences, we can put on the garments of righteousness. Because Jesus, who deserved *commendation*, received *condemnation* instead, we who deserve condemnation can receive His commendation.

At our church we say that you can summarize the gospel in four words: *Jesus in my place.*

Jesus took our sin, suffering the full weight of its penalty. In return He offers us His righteousness. When we are united to Christ, what is ours becomes His and what is His becomes ours.

> *You can summarize the gospel in four words:*
> Jesus in my place.

What Was Ours Became His; What Was His Became Ours

One of the best earthly pictures of our relationship to Christ is marriage.[11] In a marriage, all that belongs to one partner becomes the full possession of the other. My friend David Platt tells the story of his pleasant realization when he got married as a poor student that he now had access to his wife's income! Many of us can relate. When I married Veronica, I was a full-time PhD student. Which means I had no job. Which means, of course, I had very little money. Or, make that "any at all." If it weren't for the kindness of people in my church inviting me over for dinner, I would have known nothing else during those days except rice and beans and an occasional splurge of peanut butter. My bride-to-be had just obtained a job as a public school teacher—and while no one gets rich as a public school teacher, it is a full-time job and does pay a salary with benefits.

On July 28, 2000, at about 6:15 p.m., when I stood in the Lewis-Ginter Botanical Gardens in Richmond, Virginia, and said "I do" to Veronica Marie McPeters, I received, in that moment, the most beautiful bride I could have imagined, the girl who was to become the love of my life and my best friend. But I also received something else: a monthly paycheck. Her check was deposited in our joint account and I could make withdrawals whenever I wanted. And here's the great thing: I never even had to enter the classroom! She did all the work; I got to share in the money.

When you receive Christ, all that is yours becomes His, and all that is His becomes yours. He took responsibility for your sin, judgment, and corruption, and bestowed upon you His righteousness, sonship, and intimacy with the Father.[12]

Jesus + Nothing = Assurance

Our hope of heaven is based upon Jesus' finished work, plus nothing. There is nothing else that needs to be, or could be, added to what He did. I love how the old hymn says it:

> *My hope is built on nothing less, than Jesus' blood and righteousness. I dare not trust the sweetest frame, but wholly lean on Jesus' name!*

> *This is all my hope and peace—nothing but the blood of Jesus! This is all my righteousness—nothing but the blood of Jesus!*[13]

I could not be more righteous in God's eyes than I am in Christ. *In Christ,* there is nothing I could do that could make God love me more; nothing I have done that makes Him love me less.

> **In Christ, *there is nothing I could do that could make God love me more; nothing I have done that makes Him love me less.***

Maybe the clearest, most concise explanation of this is given in Paul's gospel-summary of Romans 4:5:

> But to him who does not work but believes on Him who justifies the ungodly, his faith is accounted for righteousness.

That verse has three very important phrases:

"To him who does not work": That is, to the one who realizes that there is nothing they could ever do to earn eternal life.

". . . but believes on Him who justifies the ungodly": That is, believes that God did the work necessary to save him, just like God said He did.

". . . his faith is accounted for righteousness": God counts that belief, that faith, as righteousness to us. Paul compares our belief in Christ to Abraham's belief in God's promise to give him a son. Though he was nearly one hundred, Abraham chose to believe God could bring a child from a dead womb, and God counted him as righteous for that belief (Rom. 4:3). The moment we repentantly believe God brought back the lifeless body of Jesus from the deadness of the tomb, after His offering as a payment for our sin, we are declared similarly righteous. (Rom. 4:25)

Righteousness is a free gift to all who believe that God is gracious enough to give it to them in Christ.

Righteousness is a free gift to all who believe that God is gracious enough to give it to them in Christ.

Understanding the "gift righteousness" of the gospel is a key component in obtaining assurance. If you base your assurance on what you *do* or how well you do it, you'll never find assurance. You'll always be wondering if you are doing enough. If your assurance is based on what Christ has done, however, you can rest in *His* performance. Your salvation is as secure as His finished work.

The New Testament writers all boldly declare that salvation is obtained by believing it is *done*.

But what exactly, you may wonder, does it mean to *believe*? That's where we will turn next.

4

WHAT IS BELIEF?

The rough Roman soldier knelt trembling before the apostle Paul, his forehead glistening with sweat, his eyes filled with tears of terror. An earthquake had just knocked the walls of his prison down. Pandemonium ensued, and the soldier knew he would pay with his life for the prisoners who escaped on his watch—earthquake or not. But curiously, at least one prisoner had come back.

Paul sensed God was doing something in this soldier's life, and he told him to put away his sword. "I'm not going anywhere," Paul said. "In fact, we're all still here."

"Sirs," the Roman soldier said, recalling the sermons and songs he had heard from Paul, "What must I do to be saved?"

Paul's response: "Believe on the Lord Jesus Christ, and you will be saved" (Acts 16:28–31).

Paul's words are perhaps the simplest, most straightforward explanation in the Bible of what someone must "do" to be saved: *Believe.*

Sounds simple enough. Just believe. But is that it? Mentally acknowledge that Jesus was God's Son and died on a cross for our sin? Nearly 80 percent Americans say they believe that, though for many, it makes little difference in their lives.[1] They "believe" Jesus rose from the dead like they believe Napoleon lost the battle of Waterloo. Is this all that Paul meant?

Clearly not. Jesus' half-brother, James, claims that even the demons "believe" in this way, and tremble—but we're not going to be hanging out with them in heaven (James 2:19).

Biblical belief, or "faith," includes a *volitional* aspect as well. When Jesus called the crowds in Mark 1 to "repent and believe" (Mark 1:15), He was not adding a second component to belief, but clarifying what real belief entails. Repentance is belief in action.

Repentance and belief are, biblically speaking, parts of the same whole. They are two dimensions of the same thing, two sides of the same coin.

> *Repentance and belief are, biblically speaking, parts of the same whole.*

We believe not only that Jesus lived and died; we believe He lived and died *for us* and we choose to rest our hopes for salvation upon Him. We believe not only that Jesus is Lord (as a fact of history), but that He is *our* rightful Sovereign as well, and we submit to Him (as an act of volition).

When the writer of Hebrews honors the great Old Testament heroes of faith, he identifies every single one with an *action*. Noah *constructed* an ark; Abraham *left* his home; Jacob *blessed* his grandsons; Joseph *gave instructions* concerning his bones; Moses *chose* to be mistreated; and Joshua *circled the walls of Jericho*. The great "chapter of faith" is all about *actions*. Faith is belief in action. In fact, there is no noun for faith in Hebrew, because *faith does not exist apart from its action*. Faith starts with mental assent, but if this mental assent does not lead to obedience, it is not yet "faith."

Biblical belief is the assumption of a new posture toward the Lordship of Christ and His finished work on the cross.

As I explained in the first chapter, we might express our assumption of that new posture in a "sinner's prayer"—or by "asking Jesus into our hearts," or some equivalent thereof—but just because we've prayed that prayer doesn't necessarily mean we have repented and believed.

> *Faith starts with mental assent, but if this mental assent does not lead to obedience, it is not yet "faith."*

The flip side is also true: just because we haven't prayed that prayer (or can't remember praying it) doesn't mean we haven't repented and believed. *"Repentance and belief" and "asking Jesus into our hearts" are not always interchangeable.*

Let's explore that more fully.

Reducing Salvation to a "Ceremony"?

Here is how many Christians think of "getting saved": they realize they're a sinner and they need Jesus to save them. So they approach Him and ask Him to come into their heart. Of course He says, "yes," at which time He forgives their sins, writes their names in the Lamb's Book of Life, gives them a "certificate" of salvation (a carbon copy of which is placed in their Bible), and commences a party in heaven in their honor. If they begin to doubt later whether or not they are really "saved," they replay in their minds that moment of conversion, assuring themselves of their sincerity and reminding themselves of the feelings they had after it.

Works great. At least until your memory fails you. Or if you start to wonder if you did it right. Or if you have deceived yourself into thinking something happened that really didn't. And what if you begin to ask, as I did, *Did I really feel sorry enough for my sin? Did my life change enough after I asked Him into my heart? Did I understand enough about Jesus, or my sin, or grace, when I prayed? Were there areas of rebellion I was unaware of?*

Uh-oh. Better ask Him to come into your life again. So back you go to Jesus, asking for another "certificate." You feel better for a while. But you'll probably have to do it a few more times throughout your life to be sure. The only time you think you can be absolutely assured you did it right is when you are standing face-to-face with Jesus in heaven.

The Bible depicts the moment of salvation differently. Instead of asking Jesus for a "certificate" of salvation, you start believing what God's Word says about His Lordship and His completed work at the cross. You understand that you have lived in rebellion against the rule of God and have no hope of escaping God's wrath on your own. You "kneel" in submission to His claim on your life, and rest your hope of heaven upon Him. Picture this as hopping up into His arms, submitting to go wherever He takes you, and trusting in Him to carry you into heaven.

> *If you are right now resting in His arms, knowing when you began to rest is less important than that you are doing it now.*

If at some point in the future you begin to doubt whether or not you really have put faith in Jesus, do you look backwards to try and remember that moment when you first hopped up into His arms? I suppose you could. Better, though, would be to look at where you are currently resting. If you are right now resting in His arms, knowing when you began to rest is less important than that you are doing it now. Your present posture is more important than a past memory.

Conversion is not completing a ritual, it is commencing a relationship. The assurance of ritual is based on accurate words and memory.

The assurance of relationship is based on a present posture of repentance and belief.

Present Posture Is Better Proof than a Past Memory

Here's another way to think about it: if you are seated right now, there was a point in time in which you transferred the weight of your body from your legs to the chair. You may not even remember making that decision, but the fact you are seated now proves that you did.

Salvation is a posture of repentance and faith toward the finished work of Christ in which you transfer the weight of your hopes of heaven off of your own righteousness and onto the finished work of Jesus Christ. The way to know you made the decision is by the fact you are resting in Christ now.

The apostle John almost always talks about "believing" in the present tense because it is something we do continually, not something we did once in the past (e.g., John 3:36; 9:36–38; 10:27–28; 1 John 5:13). The posture begins at a moment, but it persists for a lifetime.

The book of Leviticus provides a wonderful picture of this. Once a year each Jewish father would appear on behalf of the family to offer a sacrifice for sin. When the moment of sacrifice came, the father would lay his hand on the head of the sacrificial lamb and the priest would slit its throat. The resting of the hand of the man on the head of the lamb symbolized the transference of the guilt of the family onto the head of the sacrifice. As the lamb bled out, the guilt of the family was removed.

Faith is placing our hand upon the sacrificial head of Jesus. When we do so, Paul says, our "faith is accounted for righteousness" (Rom. 4:5). There is a moment when we first lay our hand on the head of Jesus, but faith rests its hand there for the rest of our lives. When we want to know if we are saved, we should look at where our "hand," our hope for heaven, is currently resting.

When you first assume that position of faith, you might express it in a prayer. Or you might not. The posture *is* itself a cry to God for salvation, whether you articulate that or not. But just because you prayed the prayer doesn't mean you assumed the posture, any more than telling a chair you're about to sit in it equates actually sitting down.

So, when it comes to assurance, the only real question is: *Is your hand resting on Jesus' head now?*

There Is a Moment of Salvation

As I noted in chapter 1, I don't mean to imply that there is not a "point" of salvation or that salvation is something you grow into gradually over time. Scripture depicts salvation happening in a moment: we are "born again" (John 3:1–3); our sins are washed away (Acts 22:16); Christ's righteousness is credited to us (Rom. 4:5); we are transferred from the kingdom of darkness to the kingdom of light (Col. 1:13); we go from being children of death to being beloved sons and daughters of God (Eph. 2:1–4); God's favor replaces His wrath over us (John 3:36); and we are filled with His Spirit and baptized into His body (Acts 10:44; 1 Cor. 12:13)—all in a moment. None of these are gradual evolutions.

Think again about the analogy of the chair—even if you don't remember the point at which you sat down, there was still a point at which you did. It may have been a subconscious decision, but it was a decision nonetheless. In the same way, there is a moment where you transfer your hope for heaven from your own merits to Christ's substitutionary work.

The way that you *know* you made the decision, however, is not by remembering with absolute clarity the moment you made it, but because you are seated now. Many people know exactly when that point of decision was for them. There was a dramatic moment when they submitted to Christ's Lordship and trusted in Him for salvation. Their conversion was like a wedding ceremony in which, with all of their heart, they said "yes" to Jesus. Their lives changed emphatically and they have never been the same.

For others, however, the moment is less clear. Perhaps they were raised in a Christian home, and their awareness of Jesus' Lordship grew over time. For them, it was more like they came to a point where they *realized* they believed rather than one in which they *decided* to believe.

The point is not whether we remember making the decision to get into the posture but whether we are in it now. If you remember the moment and it's very clear—great. If not—well, that's OK, too.

Either way, what we are to do now is maintain the posture of repentance and faith.

And here's the thing: If you think that you were saved in the past, but are mistaken, and what you think is a renewal of your faith turns out to be a beginning—no worries, your current posture of repentance and belief will save you even if you are mistaken about when you first assumed it.

"But wait," you say, "don't I have to ask Jesus for salvation? What if I assume the posture but don't say the prayer?" Again, the posture of repentance and faith are *in themselves* a cry for salvation. He hears the cry of your posture even if you don't voice the prayer. Nowhere does the Bible say we have to voice a prayer to be saved. The posture of repentance and belief saves.

Sometimes when you are sharing the gospel with someone it can be helpful to recount the point at which you made the decision to trust Christ so that you can urge them to make the same decision. But if you don't know the point at which you made it, you can say, "Honestly, I'm not really sure the exact moment I began to trust Christ. I know by such-and-such age I was doing it, and I know that right now I am submitted to Christ's Lordship and hoping in His finished work as my salvation. I invite you to do the same, beginning right now."

The Moment It Finally Made Sense to Me

I remember the moment this all, at last, became clear. Toward the end of my first year in college, a friend directed me to Martin Luther, whom he said had gone through his own bitter struggle with assurance. By this point I was willing to try anything. So I went to the library and checked out Luther's commentary on the book of Romans. I'll never forget that night reading his words on Romans 10:9:

> Paul says, "If thou . . . shalt believe in thine heart that God hath raised him from the dead, thou shalt be saved." That is true, for, as we read in 4:25, "Christ was delivered for our offenses, and raised again for our justification." Whoever believes these two facts will be saved. . . . We obtain the true righteousness of God *by believing sincerely the promises of God,* as we read in 4:3, "Abraham believed God, and it was counted unto him for righteousness."[2]

In that moment it, at last, all made sense. Salvation was obtained by simply resting on the two "facts" God had promised about Jesus: He was crucified as the payment for our sins; He was resurrected as proof that God accepted His sacrifice as payment. Just as Abraham was saved by believing God *would* keep His word, I was saved by believing He had.

Just as Abraham was saved by believing God would *keep His word, I was saved by believing He had.*

Those two facts were true whether I believed them or not, but when I rested my weight upon them—that is, when I placed my hopes for heaven on His finished work—they became *mine*.

The verses Luther was commenting on, Romans 10:9–10, say this:

> If you confess with your mouth the Lord Jesus and believe
> in your heart that God has raised Him from the dead, you will
> be saved. For with the heart one believes unto righteousness,
> and with the mouth confession is made unto salvation.

In these verses there are no prayers, no ceremonies. Only belief and a confession of that belief.

That night I quit analyzing an experience or a prayer and placed the hand of my soul upon the head of Jesus. Now, when I doubt whether or not I'm saved, I simply check the current location of my hand of faith. Is it on Jesus? I don't look back to the prayer I prayed with my parents when I was five, or to my rededication to Christ at sixteen. I don't even look back to the experience reading Luther's commentary. I look back two thousand years to what Christ accomplished on Calvary. And I rest upon what He finished there.

Don't try to find assurance from a prayer you prayed in the past; find assurance by resting in the present on what *Jesus did* in the past. If you are resting right now in what Jesus did two thousand years ago to save you, then, if never before, you are saved at this moment, even *if you don't signify it with a prayer*. It is the *relationship* to Christ that saves, not the prayer that signified the beginning of that relationship. When you started to rest is not as important as the fact that you are doing it now.

Do you believe that Jesus has paid it all? Do you know that He is Lord, and are you in a posture of submission to that Lordship? Then rest in Him.

Leading My Kids to Jesus

As a father of four young children, I have often reflected on the best way to lead them to faith. I want their decision to follow Jesus to be significant, but I also don't want them to go through what I went through. I know that when you present kids with a "Don't you want to be a good girl and accept Jesus and not go to a fiery hell?" of course they say, "Yes." "Praying the prayer" in such a situation may have little do with actual faith in Christ and have more to do with making Daddy happy.

I know that when you present kids with a "Don't you want to be a good girl and accept Jesus and not go to a fiery hell?" of course they say, "Yes."

For that reason, many parents don't want to *push* their child to make a decision for Christ. What if we coerce them into praying a prayer they don't understand, and that keeps them from really dealing with the issues later when they really understand it? Might having them pray the prayer too early on inoculate them from really coming to Jesus later, giving them false assurance that keeps them from dealing with their need to be saved?

I understand that fear. At the same time, I know that children are capable of faith. (In fact, Jesus tells adults that for them to be saved they must become like children, not vice versa!) And Jesus says that those of us who make it difficult for little kids to put faith in Him ought to have a millstone tied around our necks and be thrown into the sea (Matt. 18:1–6). So I don't ever want to discourage my kids from faith.

The dilemma is resolved, however, by seeing salvation as a posture toward Christ and not as a ceremony. *There is only one posture ever appropriate to Christ: surrendered to His Lordship, and believing that He did what He said He did.* From the very beginning of their lives, I want my kids to assume that posture!

Why would I ever want them to have a different posture toward Christ? The opposite of believing is unbelieving; the opposite of surrendered is rebellious. So I teach my children, all along the way, to be surrendered toward Jesus and believing of what He said He accomplished.

I explain to them often what Christ has done and encourage them to pin their hopes of righteousness on His work and not theirs. Whenever they think about their hopes for heaven, I want their minds to go to what Jesus did on Calvary. And from the first time I began to speak to my kids about Jesus, I presented Him as Lord. It was literally the first thing I whispered in their ears when they were born. Over the years I have told them that if they would trust in Christ's finished work as their own, and follow Him as Lord, they would be saved.

But what if they don't really grasp all that salvation entails? What if they don't really know exactly why they are leaning upon Him, why they need His grace? Certainly, as my kids grow older, they will have moments of insight in which they understand better His grace, and defining moments in which they "own" their posture toward Him. But it is a posture I can encourage them toward from the beginning. *Again: only one posture is ever appropriate toward Christ: repentant and believing.*

To be honest, I'd even be OK if they ended up not knowing the precise moment they "received Christ." What a great evidence of the grace of God to be able to say, "For as long as I can remember, I have recognized the Lordship of Jesus and believed that He did what He said He did."

Children that grow up in unbelieving homes will likely have a memorable conversion to Christ where they pass from darkness to light. But I want my kids to *grow up* in the light. Personally,

> **Only one posture is ever appropriate toward Christ: repentant and believing.**

I'd prefer they NOT have an "exciting" testimony that involves years or rebellion, foolishness, and unbelief. I want each of my kids to have a nice, "boring" testimony; to be kids who spend their whole lives enraptured with what God did for them in Jesus. If and when they do have a season of rebellion, I'll pray for a dramatic conversion, or rededication, or whatever you want to call it. But for now, I pray they'll always look toward our Savior in submission and faith.

Children that grow up in unbelieving homes will likely have a memorable conversion to Christ where they pass from darkness to light. But I want my kids to grow up in the light.

The bottom line: It's never too young to begin trusting in and surrendering to Jesus.

The gospel has been announced! Jesus has summoned the whole world to repent and believe. That includes our children. I want them to obey *today*.

Assurance Is Impossible Unless You Believe Salvation Is by Faith Alone

In recent years, many Bible-believing Christians have downplayed the centrality of "justification by faith alone" in the gospel message because, they say, following Jesus means so much more than simply "accepting" a gift of salvation. Following Jesus means adopting his lifestyle and committing yourself wholly to His kingdom mission.

It is true that following Jesus is about much more than accepting a gift. A dramatic change of life and radical commitment to the mission is always the fruit of a heart changed by faith. However, if the idea of gift-righteousness given through faith alone is discarded, so will be the possibility of assurance. If our response to Jesus' offer of salvation becomes "adopting new kingdom realities" or "committing yourself to the mission of Jesus," the question of "how much is enough?" will be inescapable. We will be plagued with the question of whether we've been committed *enough* to the mission, sorry *enough* for our sin, or living *sufficiently* by kingdom principles.

The Reformer Martin Luther, recognizing this, said that apart from salvation by faith alone there could be no real assurance of peace with God. The righteousness God gives us in salvation, Luther said, is a "passive" righteousness, meaning we do nothing to obtain but receive it, by faith.

In the preface to his *Commentary on Galatians,* Luther says,

> "This most excellent righteousness—that of faith, . . . is passive. We do nothing in the matter; we give nothing to God but simply receive and allow someone else to work in us.
>
> Nothing comforts our conscience so firmly as this passive righteousness. . . . When I see a person who is bruised enough already being oppressed with the law, terrified with sin, and thirsting for comfort, it is time for me to remove the law and active righteousness from his sight and set before him, by the gospel, the Christian and passive righteousness...
>
> So then do we do nothing to obtain this righteousness? No, nothing at all. Perfect righteousness is to do nothing, to hear nothing, to know nothing of the law or of works, but to know and believe only that Christ has gone to the Father and is no longer visible; that he sits in heaven at the right hand of his Father, not as a judge, but is made by God our wisdom, righteousness, holiness, and redemption; in short, that he is our high priest, entreating for us and reigning over us and in us by grace.
>
> The church is founded upon, and consists in, this doctrine alone."[3]

For more on why the doctrine of "justification by faith alone" is indispensable for gaining assurance, including an explanation of passages commonly assured to mean that good works are also necessary to obtain salvation, see Appendix 2.

Assurance comes from seeing that our righteous standing before God—Christ himself—is seated securely in heaven at the Father's right hand. There He rests, and there upon Him rests our hand of faith.[4]

Belief is the hand that lays hold of the *finished* work of Jesus. Spirit-generated belief will always result in a new heart—a heart that loves good works and pursues them for Jesus' sake. It is impossible for Spirit-generated faith to not lead to these good works, so if they are absent, so is genuine faith. These good works are not, however, the same thing as the faith itself. Faith's sole object is the finished work of Christ. Faith cannot rest in the good works it produces. Faith cannot rest in itself. Faith that looks anywhere else but Christ will find not assurance but incessant doubt. Only by resting entirely in his finished work can the troubled soul find peace.

Paul's words to the Philippian jailor were simple and sufficient: *"Believe on the Lord Jesus Christ and you shall be saved."* Believing on the Lord Jesus Christ means acknowledging, submissively, that Christ is the Lord and that He accomplished our salvation, just as He said He did— and resting our hopes there.

Another word the Gospel writers use to summarize this response is *repentance*. As I'll show you in the next chapter, repentance is not something we do in addition to believing, but rather a component of true believing. It highlights what we do with the facts we believe about Jesus. It is the breath in the body of true faith, the other side of the coin of belief.

5

WHAT IS
REPENTANCE?

The young politician was genuinely learning to admire Jesus. He was fascinated by the message of this enigmatic, but wonderful, teacher. For many years he had been aware that something was missing from his life, and he was convinced he had finally found the missing piece. During an Easter service at the exciting, growing church he attended, he prayed to receive Jesus and was baptized the next week.

Immediately he got into a small group and started to volunteer at his church. He tried to bring "God" into government. He brought his family and many of his coworkers to church. He donated significant amounts of money to Christian causes, eventually giving so much money to his church that the new gymnasium was named after him. In later years, he served as an elder.

And when he died, he went to hell.

Does this sound impossible, even absurd, to you? Me, too. Yet, the Gospel of Mark describes just such a man. A seeker of Jesus, a "rich, young ruler of the Jews," came to Jesus, expressing an earnest desire to be His follower. We know that he was moral, responsible, and respectable. And he had a clear interest in Jesus. Mark tells us that Jesus loved him.

But there was something about him—something in his heart that Jesus saw; something invisible to everyone else. The man *loved* his money. He worshipped it. He would be willing to share some of it, no doubt, but he would never be able to let God take its place. He would be able to look and act Christian—very Christian, in fact—but he'd never fully follow Jesus. There would always be conditions, exceptions, and limitations to what he'd do and where he'd go.

Jesus exposed all this with one, simple demand: "One thing you lack: Go your way, sell whatever you have and give to the poor, and you will have treasure in heaven; and come take up the cross, and follow Me" (Mark 10:21). Sadly, the young seeker walked away and, as far as we know, never came back.

Because you and I can't see into another's heart like that, we can't make that same demand of those coming to Jesus. Nowhere in Scripture do the Apostles demand people actually sell all their possessions to follow Jesus. What this story makes clear, however, is that when we come to Jesus nothing can be off-limits. We cannot come with preconditions or limitations. To possess eternal life, we must be willing to let everything else go. We don't approach Jesus to negotiate eternal life; we approach Him in total surrender. As C. S. Lewis famously said, "We don't come to Him as bad people trying to become good people; we come as rebels to lay down our arms."[1]

Jesus said:

> "Whoever of you does not forsake all that he has cannot be My disciple." (Luke 14:33)

> "If anyone comes to Me and does not hate his father and mother, wife and children, brothers and sisters, yes, and his own life also, he cannot be My disciple." (Luke 14:26)

His words are strong to the point of bewilderment. *"Hate my father and mother . . . my wife, even my own children?"* Doesn't the Bible command us to love and honor these?

Jesus could not have meant "hate" in the sense of despising them or desiring their harm, as this would contradict His other teachings to love and honor our parents, lay down our lives for our spouses, and desire the good of all people, even our enemies. Rather, He is saying that we must be so committed to Him that by comparison even our most intimate relationships *look like* hate. There can be no question where ultimate authority and the corresponding allegiance lies.

When my first daughter was born we had a family dog. I loved the dog. I took care of the dog and fed the dog. Had I been put in a situation, however, where I had to choose between the life of the dog and the life of my daughter, without any hesitation I would have chosen my daughter. Compared to my love for my daughter, my love for that dog looked like "hate."

> *"We don't come to Him as bad people trying to become good people; we come as rebels to lay down our arms."*
> *(C. S. Lewis)*

This recognition that Jesus is the absolute Lord is called "repentance." It is the only right posture toward God. It was the first response Jesus called for in His preaching of the gospel (Mark 1:15); the first word out of Peter's mouth in his first recorded sermon in Acts (Acts 2:38); and what Paul said God had commanded all men everywhere to do now that Jesus had been resurrected (Acts 17:30).[2] Apart from repentance there can be no reconciliation to God.

Repentance is not subsequent to belief; it is part of belief. It is belief in action—choices that flow out of conviction. *Repentance* literally means "a change of mind" (in Greek, *metanoia; meta*—"new"; *noia*—"mind") about Jesus. Repentance is not merely changing your actions; it is changing your actions because you have changed your attitude about Jesus' authority and glory. So closely linked are belief and repentance that the Bible uses them interchangeably: "Whoever *believes* in the Son has eternal life; whoever does not *obey* the Son shall not see life" (John 3:36 ESV).

Repentance doesn't mean you begin to be greatly influenced by Jesus, or that you reform a lot of your ways. If you follow Jesus in 99 percent of His teachings but deliberately hold back 1 percent, you have not repented. You are still choosing which 99 percent to surrender and which 1 percent to keep, which means you are still in charge. You haven't really *changed your mind* about Jesus.

Repentance means recognizing that Jesus is *Lord*; you have no more say in the matter. You recognize that He is the absolute, rightful Ruler of the universe, and that those who have lived as their own authority have committed cosmic treason against Him. Simple enough, right?

Not in reality. Because let's be honest: who is there that can say that they are, in reality, 100 percent surrendered to Jesus—that He calls the shots in all areas of their lives? It seems that every day God uncovers some new area in my life that He does not yet control! And didn't even the greatest saints have blind spots and areas of hypocrisy? Didn't Peter *deny* Jesus at one point? The Gospels are filled with stories of disciples of weak, faltering faith.[3] King David committed adultery and murder and then lied about it for several months, yet never ceased being God's beloved, a man after God's own heart.

We need, it seems, more clarity first on what repentance *is not* in order to draw some firm conclusions about what it *is*.

What Repentance Is Not

Simply Praying a Sinner's Prayer

Repentance is not simply praying a prayer that acknowledges our sinfulness and asks for forgiveness. Nor is it walking an aisle, signing a card, or giving a public testimony. Repentance is not fundamentally a motion of the hands, mouth or feet; it is a motion of the heart in which we abandon our posture of rebellion and adopt one of submission toward Christ. Repentance is *evidenced* by outward action, but it does not equal that.

Feeling Sorry about Our Sin

Shedding tears over sin does not equal repentance. The apostle Paul says in 2 Corinthians 7:10, "For godly sorrow produces repentance leading to salvation, not to be regretted; but the sorrow of the world produces death." There is, according to Paul, a "sorrow of the world" that might well produce tears and yet have nothing to do with repentance. Perhaps they are tears of shame, regret, or self-pity. Or the embarrassment of being caught. These emotions might eventually lead to repentance, but they are not, in and of themselves, repentance.

John the Baptist told his hearers to "bear fruits worthy of repentance" (Luke 3:8), and then provided them with a list of examples, including honest dealings, kindness, generosity, and proper worship. He equated repentance not simply with new emotions, but new actions. Those who did not bring forth these kinds of fruits would be "cut down and thrown into the fire" (3:9). Those whose sorrow for their sin does not result in a change of actions have not repented.

Confession of Sin

Confessing our sin, even in great detail and with great emotion, does not equal repentance. Many people weep their way through a confession but go right back to their sin. Their confession is not a "change of mind" about their sin; it's more of an emotional catharsis.

Here's the thing: an emotional catharsis may *feel* redemptive. It feels good to tell a friend, or a pastor or priest, where you messed up and have him tell you it's all going to be OK, that you are still a good person. Their affirmation, however, cannot reestablish your relationship to God. Only Jesus can do that. Our tears do not wash away our sin. Only Jesus' blood does. Salvation is not about making you feel better but about actually removing your condemnation before God.

In the years I spent as a youth pastor, I remember seeing high school girls weep huge tears of regret at youth camp, usually on Thursday night, the last night of camp. By that time the students had averaged about three hours of sleep each night for three nights straight, and the preacher had saved his best sermon for the final night. The band played everyone's favorite songs. Toward the end of the Thursday night service an emotional dam would break—I'd see a girl in the middle of the third row start crying because she felt ashamed about something she'd done and terrified that her parents would find out about

> *Our tears do not wash away our sin. Only Jesus' blood does.*

it. For high school girls, tears work something like yawns: seeing someone else do it suddenly makes you want to. So the girl next to her would start crying. The girl beside her started crying because their tears remind her how lonely she is. And on and on down the line. Soon the entire cadre would be down front weeping and confessing their sins and promising to be missionaries and not date until they were thirty. They'd hold hands walking back to their cabin, singing "Kumbayah," and talk late into the evening about how awesome it is to be a Christian. Their change of heart usually lasted till about ten o'clock the next morning, when they'd forget about it until the next year when they came back to youth camp and went through the same process again. Rinse and repeat.

We must be particularly careful to clarify confession and repentance, because confession can *feel* purifying. Many people are looking for exoneration, be that from a friend, a spouse, a counselor, a pastor, or Jesus. They just want someone to tell them they're "OK." Biblical repentance, however, is not merely a request for exoneration; it is a change of heart about our sin. Even confession of our sin to Jesus, soaked with tears, but apart from a change of attitude toward our sin, will not bring about eternal life. Confession is part of the repentance process, but not the sum total of it.

Godly sorrow, Paul says, leads to life. Godly sorrow is the fruit of a changed heart. That kind of sorrow is not measured by the amount of tears but the change in direction. James says that faith without *works* is dead, not faith without tears. Faith is shown, he says, by its works.[4]

Getting Religious

Getting religious does not equal repentance. Religious activity is, in fact, one of the most common *substitutes* for genuine repentance. Religious activity can be an attempt to "pay God off" in order to keep Him at a distance or to conceal the true state of our hearts, as if we can purchase latitude for the lifestyle we want to continue. "I've gone to church so much," or "I've done so many other good things recently," we think, "God won't be that bothered if I do this again just this once." That shows we've had no change of heart about our sin; we've simply worked out a formula (we think) to keep God off our backs.

King Saul tried something similar in order to cover up his rebellious defiance of God by offering a sacrifice—a quite costly one, in fact. The prophet Samuel responded to his extravagant sacrifice:

"Has the LORD as great delight in burnt offering and sacrifices, as in obeying the voice of the LORD? Behold, to obey is better than sacrifice, and to listen than the fat of rams." (1 Sam. 15:22 ESV)

A cheating man who buys his wife expensive gifts is not addressing his unfaithfulness but covering it up. His purchase of gifts is an attempt to alleviate his conscience or to keep his wife deluded about the true state of his heart.

In one of Flannery O'Connor's novels, *Wise Blood*, she describes a character with "a deep black wordless conviction . . . that the way to avoid sin was to avoid Jesus."[5] In other words, he thought that by keeping his life in a relatively "clean" state he could avoid having to deal with God altogether. This is the devil's religious substitute for genuine repentance.

Repentance is not securing a pardon before God so that we can go on sinning with impunity; it is a choice to submit to God and to seek ceasing from sin entirely.[6] Repentance doesn't mean we amend our behavior, it means we begin to pursue God's will with abandon.

Partial Surrender

Repentance is not a partial surrender in which we let Jesus take control of certain areas but not others. Jesus said following Him meant "denying ourselves" and "taking up our cross." It is important to note that He didn't give us a list of things to deny; He said we must deny *our very selves,* that is, the center of our desires, decision-making faculties, and source of identity. In those days, "taking up the cross" would have meant forfeiting any hold on your life.

My childhood Sunday school teacher used to say it like this, "In every heart there is a throne and a cross. If Christ is on the throne, self must be on the cross. But if self is on the throne, Christ will be on the cross."

Imagine if I proudly announced to my wife that during the next year I would be 95 percent faithful to her. Now, that is an A- at even the strictest colleges. My wife, however, would not be excited. That means out of one hundred girls I know, I plan to be sexually involved with five of them. That is not an "A-" faithfulness rating; that is wholly unfaithful.

You don't follow Jesus like you follow someone on Twitter, where you are free to take or leave their thoughts at your leisure. Following Jesus is not letting Him come into your life to be an influence, even if it's a significant influence. Following Jesus means submitting to Him in all areas at all times regardless of whether you agree with what He says or not.

Jesus comes into our lives as "Lord," or not at all. When I was in high school, a popular bumper sticker boasted, "Jesus is my Copilot." I suppose that meant Jesus was there to help them when they got into a jam. How backwards. If Jesus is your copilot, somebody is in the wrong seat. It's His car, and we stole it. Repentance means abandoning the driver's seat and asking, "Jesus, where are we going?" He doesn't come to join us in our stolen vehicle, hoping to make chummy conversation, advise us about the most desirable routes, or help us with car trouble. He comes to reclaim what we've stolen from Him.

Many people relate to Jesus like I do the little British woman that lives in the dashboard of my car. I tell her where I'd like to go and she advises me on the best route. If I decide to ignore her counsel, she patiently says "recalculating" and adjusts herself to my new choices. (One of my worst marital moments was when my wife and I were in a small tussle and I said, "Why can't you be more like that British woman? When I don't do what she wants, she doesn't nag me, she just patiently adjusts herself to my new plans." My wife did not respond positively, and neither does Jesus to people who attempt to treat Him that way.) Jesus won't come as your copilot or your homeboy. He comes as your Lord and Master. As Jared Wilson says, "The only deal with Jesus He's willing to make is His righteousness for your guilt and absolute surrender."[7] It is an unbelievable deal for us, but it is one that requires we go all-in.

Perfection

Perhaps by this point you are feeling overwhelmed. You are saying, "But who can honestly claim that Jesus is Lord over all their life? Who can say that their repentance ushered them into a life of perfection—with no inconsistencies?"

Not Peter, who, after walking with Jesus for three years, denied Him three times in the space of one evening. Peter continued to struggle with hypocrisy, cowardice, and racism even after being filled with the Holy Spirit and becoming one of Christianity's greatest preachers. His inconsistency got so bad at one point that Paul had to rebuke him publicly![8]

> *Many people relate to Jesus like I do the little British woman that lives in the dashboard of my car. I tell her where I'd like to go and she advises me on the best route.*

Not King David, the adulterer, murderer, and cover-up artist, who did all these things *after* he was called "the man after God's own heart" and writing a lot of those great Psalms. Not Job, who lost his patience with God and had to be rebuked by Him for challenging His wisdom (Job 40:1–5; 42:1–6).

Not the disciples of Jesus who deserted Him at the hour of Jesus' trial. Not Martin Luther, the great Reformer, who by his own admission, cursed and drank too much and ended his life as a virulent anti-Semite. Not John Wesley, one of the primary leaders of America's Great Awakening, who had a terrible marriage, due largely to his own selfishness, or A. W. Tozer, who seems to have had the same problem.

Not even Paul, who talked about his never-ending, discouraging struggle with sin. His pride, he said, was so out of control that God had to send him a thorn in the flesh to humble him.[9] He admitted of his own heart:

> For I delight in the law of God according to the inward
> man. But I see another law in my members, warring against the
> law of my mind, and bringing me into captivity to the law of
> sin which is in my members. O wretched man that I am! Who
> will deliver me from this body of death? (Rom. 7:22–24)

I know well Paul's feeling here. I certainly cannot say my repentance has resulted in a life of perfect consistency. I know what it's like to fall for the hundredth time to the same sin and wonder how God could possibly call you "His."

If repentance were perfection, none of these people repented. Repentance, however, means recognizing Jesus' authority and submitting to it, even though you know your heart is weak, divided, and pulled in conflicting directions. Repentance includes a plea for God to change your inconsistent, divided heart (Ps. 86:11; Mark 9:24).

Yes, Jesus turned away the rich, young ruler because He saw that man had a determination to hold onto his money regardless of what Jesus commanded. But many of those whom Jesus received in the Gospels came with fear and doubting. Many continued to struggle with those inconsistencies long after they came to Jesus. Yet Jesus not only welcomed them, He *commended* many of them for their great faith and future promise.

One disciple, Joseph of Arimathea, was actually on the council that condemned Jesus to death. While he did not consent to Jesus' death, his opposition was relatively quiet. In fact, John calls him a "secret disciple," and says that he kept his faith secret, at least at first, because he was afraid. But he was still called a disciple![10] And the Gospels of Luke and John present his quiet act of securing Jesus' body as a commendable act of faith.

Another man in the Gospels had the audacity to ask Jesus for a miracle and then admit that he wasn't even sure Jesus could actually do it.[11] Even with this faltering faith, Jesus did the miracle for him.

I have no doubts the Holy Spirit recorded stories like these in the New Testament so that we would understand genuine repentance does not mean we live with perfect consistency.

What Repentance *Is*

So now we may be in a place to understand better what repentance *is*. Let me draw a few conclusions:

Repentance Is Not the Absence of Struggle; It Is the Absence of Settled Defiance

Repentance is acknowledging that Jesus is Lord of everything as a matter of who He is. Whatever your disagreement with Jesus, He is right and you are wrong—be that your position on abortion, sex before marriage, homosexuality, generosity, or anything else. While you may not understand all of His ways yet, you recognize that He makes the rules. Period. It means you do the things He says. Jesus said, "Why do you call Me 'Lord, Lord,' and not do the things which I say?" (Luke 6:46).

While we continue to wrestle with our divided hearts, the trajectory has been set and the winner of the argument has been declared. We struggle toward the goal. We fall more than we stand, especially at first, and crawl more than we run. We often find our hearts consumed more with unbelief than belief.

Underneath the struggle, however, is the understanding that Jesus is right and we are yielded to following where He leads. While our flesh resists His authority, our heart consents.

Don't you hear that in Paul's statement in Romans 7:22–24?

"With my mind I serve the law of God 'while in my body' I feel like a captive to sin" (Rom. 7:25). That is certainly an accurate description of my struggle. Even though my flesh wars against Him, my innermost being delights in God and is submissive to Him. Perhaps you say, "But sometimes I don't delight in God, sometimes I delight more in sin!" But deep down do you at least *desire to desire* God? That is where it begins.

Think about this: belief in the gospel is not demonstrated by "never falling" but by what you do *when* you fall. Paul fell often but each time he got back up looking toward God, thanking God for forgiveness and that the process Jesus had started in him that he was sure to complete (Rom. 7:25; Phil. 1:6).

When those who believe the gospel fall, they renew their posture of repentance, re-embrace the gift-righteousness of Christ, thank God for the promise of their victory, and *get back up*. Those who do not believe the gospel wallow in their failure. They soar with pride when they are doing well; but plunge into despair when they falter.

I love how the book of Proverbs says it, "A righteous man may fall seven times, and rise again" (24:16). The righteous man is not one who never falls, but one who always gets back up. If you are watching a man walk through the mall and he falls, you

> *Belief in the gospel is not demonstrated by "never falling" but by what you do when you fall.*

snigger and point it out to your friends. If he does it twice and looks like he is about to do it again, you get out your phone, record it, and send it to your friends who aren't there. If he does it a fourth and fifth time, you post it on YouTube and it goes viral. If he falls a seventh time, you conclude there is something wrong with him and feel bad for posting it on YouTube. Yet God says righteous people fall seven times. Righteous people fall so much that it sometimes seems they can barely walk! But each time they get back up looking at Jesus.

Faith is not the absence of doubt; it is continuing to follow Jesus in the midst of doubt. Imagine a person who's never seen civilization being suddenly asked to get on board a plane so they can travel with their infant to a remote hospital where they can obtain a needed medicine. Everything in them screams out in fear. Yet they drag themselves, kicking and screaming, onto the plane. Though their whole being resists it, their desire to save their infant overcomes their fears, and they get on board.

Repentance often works the same way: we put to death our desires, fears, and confusion because we know that Jesus is more important than them all. Like Peter said to Jesus, after a particularly difficult teaching in which many departed from Jesus and Jesus asked the disciples, "Do you also want to go away?" Peter says, "To whom shall we go? You have the words of eternal life" (John 6:67–68). Peter doesn't say, "Of course not! What You're saying makes perfect sense." He says, essentially, "I don't understand You on this either, Jesus, but there's no way I'm following my doubts if they lead away from You. So I'll follow You even with my doubts. You're worth the risk."

Likewise, we continue to follow Jesus as we struggle with sin. *Repentance ushers us into a life of greater struggle, not out of one.* While I've heard of some people who were immediately released from certain sinful desires, like alcoholism, anger, or same-sex attraction when they received Christ, as a pastor of fifteen years I can say that that is not the normal experience of new believers. Christians, like the apostle Paul, continue to struggle with sin, often unsuccessfully, for the rest of their lives. *The struggle is proof of their new nature.* They fall often, but when they do, they always get up looking His direction.

Repentance, therefore, is not the absence of struggle; it is the absence of settled defiance. No category exists in the Gospels for those who "receive Jesus" as Savior but not Lord. But thankfully—mercifully— there is a huge space for those who struggle and backslide.[12]

Repentance Is Not Just about Stopping Sin but Also Starting to Follow Jesus

Many people interpret repentance as merely stopping bad things, to cease and desist the breaking of the commandments. Jesus, however, called us to be His *disciples*, which means actively pursuing His agenda and mission:

> "Whoever desires to come after Me, let him deny himself,
> and take up his cross, and follow Me. For whoever desires to
> save his life will lose it, but whoever loses his life for My sake
> and the gospel's will save it." (Mark 8:34–35)

Engaging in the mission was not a special calling that a few special followers received after many years, like Obedience 2.0 or "Platinum Medallion Discipleship." It was inherent in the very first call to follow.[13] It was for *anyone* who would come after Jesus.

Are you actively engaged in the Great Commission, using your spiritual gifts to pursue God's purposes on earth?

In the Old Testament, the prophet Micah said,

> He has shown you, O man, what is good; and what does
> the LORD require of you but to *do justly*, to *love mercy*, and to
> *walk humbly with your God*? (Mic. 6:8, emphasis added)

And Moses said,

> And now, Israel, what does the LORD your God require of
> you, but to fear the LORD your God, to walk in *all His ways* and
> to love Him, to serve the LORD your God with all your heart
> and with all your soul, and to keep the commandments of the
> LORD and His statutes? (Deut. 10:12–13, emphasis added)

Following Jesus is about walking with Him. Walking with Him is
about loving Him, serving Him, and pursuing His justice and mercy on
earth. Discipleship is not a passive posture in which we stop a few bad
things. We must start a bunch of really good ones as well.[14] Have you
become regular in your church? Are you discovering your spiritual gifts?
Are you giving financially, sacrificially for the mission?

Repentance Involves a Spirit-Fueled Change of Desires

We'll get more into this in chapter 7, but conversion includes an
actual, Spirit-induced change of desires. Repentance is, in its essence, a
Spirit-generated change of mind.

The moment of salvation includes what theologians call "regeneration" in which God renews our hearts into His image. This is what Paul
was referring to when he said,

> If anyone is in Christ, he is a new creation; old things
> have passed away; behold, all things have become new. (2 Cor.
> 5:17)

At conversion, God changes your spiritual appetites. You begin to
hunger for righteousness, not sin. Christ becomes more to you than simply a figure of history or a distant ruler. He becomes a Father you cherish
and a Friend you treasure. Fascination with "old things" begins to fade in
the all-surpassing glory of Christ.

This change of desires is first evidenced by your choice to follow Jesus. Apart from the Spirit's enlightening work, you'd never choose to forsake all to follow Christ. No matter how many times you were offered the choice, you'd always choose to stay in sin. Think of it like this: A man is standing on the ledge of a skyscraper convinced he is a bird. You approach him from behind, offering him the chance to come back down to safety. He will never receive your offer because he is convinced that he can fly. Every single time you offer him the choice, he'll choose to jump. But imagine you had the ability to inject him with a serum that would restore his sanity. Now, in his right mind, you extend to him the same choice. Without any compulsion, he receives your offer. Every single time.

In both cases the choice was his, but the "free" choice was reflective of the sanity of his mind. Our choice to repent and believe always reflects God's prior work inside of us. It is God who works in us, Paul says, not only to do, but also *to will to do,* for God's good pleasure (Phil. 2:13).

This is not to downplay the active role we must play in repentance. While God is the one who changes our desires, we are the ones who make the choice to submit. Many people feel the pull of God on their hearts and resist it, and Jesus places the blame for that squarely upon their shoulders. To the unbelieving Jews in the first century, He doesn't say, "I never gathered you," but "how many times I gathered you but you would not come!"[15]

Honestly, how this works together—God enabling us to choose and us making the choice—I'm not quite sure. But I do know that if you desire in any way to make that choice right now, it is the result of God working in you.[16] I also know that if you want to make that choice right now, you are free to. (And, even if you are divided about whether or not you "want" to make the choice, you are still free to. Don't sit around waiting on Jesus to do something else in your heart before you make the choice. He demands you do it today whether you feel like it or not. And just like Jesus received those in the Gospels filled with doubts and divided hearts, He will receive you, too.)

It is because repentance involves a Spirit-fueled change of desires that repentance and faith are, in their essence, not two separate acts, but one, two sides of the same coin. We turn from sin only *because* we see that God is greater than sin. Faith in God is synonymous with "dis-faith" in something else. The Thessalonians, Paul said, turned *from* their idols to the living God (1 Thess. 1:9).

Charles Spurgeon, British pastor of the nineteenth century, summarized it like this:

> Instead of saying, "It [repentance] is only a change of mind," it seems to me more truthful to say it is a great and deep change—even a change of the mind itself.[17]

When the mind has truly been changed, repentance is the natural and inevitable result.

So how do you tell if that change of heart has happened to you? Again, it's not because you cease sinning altogether or lose all desire to sin. We will wrestle with the flesh until the day we die. If you have been awakened to the need for God and the realization that you cannot go into eternity independent of Jesus, that *in itself* is a Spirit-granted revelation (John 16:8–9). So is the recognition that Jesus is the Lord and that to stand in opposition to Him is insanity (1 Cor. 12:3; Prov. 1:7).

Furthermore, the evidences of this change don't occur all at once—as in one split second you begin to despise extramarital sex and develop a deep passion for Bible study, long hours of prayer, and Christian contemporary music. While justification (God declaring you legally righteous because of the finished work of Christ) and the new birth (God placing

His living, resurrecting Holy Spirit into your heart) happen all at once, the passions of godliness grow in you only over time.

As I noted earlier, sometimes the desire in our innermost being that Paul speaks of begins merely as a desire for that desire. Be encouraged: a desire to desire God is the first echo of a heart awakened to God.

The gospel, in that sense, is like a seed that starts small but blossoms into a mighty tree.[18] Don't grow discouraged at how slowly the plant seems to be growing. Quit focusing on that and focus on Jesus instead. Resting in His completed work is what grows you the fastest. If you dig up a seed you've planted every few days to analyze its progress, not only will you be discouraged at how slowly it is progressing, you'll probably impede its growth as well. But let that seed abide in the soil and soon enough it will be a flourishing tree. In fact, persevering in confidence even when you don't "feel" the growth is part of the faith process.

So keep your eyes on Jesus. Water the seed of new life in your heart with the word of the gospel. Rejoice daily in the fact that God's acceptance of you is not based on how much spiritual fruit you've produced but on Christ's finished work. Keep gazing upon that truth or, as Jesus phrased it, *abide* in it, and you will bear much

> *Water the seed of new life in your heart with the word of the gospel.*

fruit.[19] The seed of the gospel, Jesus said, will sprout into a harvest so plentiful it will blow your mind. Paul said it would be beyond all we could even imagine or ask for.[20]

A Divine Mystery: Jesus Repented in My Place

I close this chapter with one other thought about repentance I find to be both comforting and deeply mysterious.

During my freshman year of college, as I scoured the Bible to determine what qualified as "real" repentance, I could not escape the questions: "How could I ever repent enough to be truly worthy of Jesus? How could I ever give a sufficient response to His Lordship? How could I ever be sorry enough for my sin?" Even my best repentance, my fullest surrender, was a far cry from what was due unto Jesus! I knew God could never look at me and say, "Your repentance was perfect! You were sorry enough for your sin. You gave due weight to My glory."

That thought kept me from peace. But then I came across N. T. Wright's explanation of the odd little story of Jesus' baptism in Matthew 3:1–17.[21] John the Baptist was offering a "baptism of repentance." Jews, Roman soldiers, and sinners of all stripes were coming to him to be baptized, repenting of their sins. As they were baptized, symbolizing their repentance toward God, John would command them, "Therefore bear fruits worthy of repentance" (3:8).

One afternoon, Jesus stepped into the water, requesting baptism. John objected, understandably: "Why do *You* need to undergo a 'baptism of repentance'?" Indeed! What did Jesus have to repent of? He had never sinned!

Jesus told John, however, not to resist Him, for He was doing it "to fulfill all righteousness" (Matt. 3:15).

Whose righteousness would that baptism fulfill? *His* righteousness was already fulfilled, and could not be any fuller! It was *my* righteousness he was fulfilling. He was undergoing a baptism of repentance in my place, repenting in a way that could truly be called "righteous," so that His death could be a perfect substitute for mine.

He lived the life I should have lived. All of it. He did everything perfectly in my place. So the good news for me is that I don't have to repent *perfectly*, because He did so for me. As the Puritans used to say, "Even our tears of repentance must be washed in the blood of the Lamb."

This does not negate that when we come to Christ there must be a recognition of, and submissiveness toward, His Lordship. It simply takes off of us the weight of feeling like we have to repent perfectly in a way that earns His approval. Jesus earned it. Believe that and submit to it.

The Anglican pastor Augustus Montague Toplady must have sensed this when in 1763 he wrote, "Could my zeal no respite know, could my tears forever flow, all for sin could not atone; Thou must save, and Thou alone . . . Rock of Ages, cleft for me, let me hide myself in Thee!"

Hallelujah, what a Savior!

Have You Really Repented?

So have you really repented of your sin? Perhaps you have prayed a prayer, walked an aisle, or been involved in all kinds of religious activities, but you have never taken seriously the Lordship of Christ. Your life has never really changed because your attitude toward the Lordship of Christ has not changed.

I've often heard it said that many "Christians" will miss heaven by eighteen inches, the distance between their heads and their hearts. Don't let that be you. Let what you know to be true about Christ captivate your soul and command your behavior. Repent.

Make the choice to (in the words of John Piper) "replace all God-dishonoring, Christ-belittling perceptions and dispositions and purposes with God-treasuring, Christ-exalting ones."[22]

IF "ONCE SAVED, ALWAYS SAVED," WHY DOES THE BIBLE SEEM TO WARN US SO OFTEN ABOUT LOSING OUR SALVATION?

I was taught to share the gospel by means of the "gospel tract." If you're unfamiliar with one of those, think of it as a short, tri-fold pamphlet that explains the basic points of the gospel and calls for a response. My church had a whole rack of them, ranging from the "no-nonsense, give-it-to-me-alliterated" version to the "friendly newspaper comic strip" version to the "fake ten-dollar bill with the 'here's a real tip, trust Jesus'" version. "Chick tracts" were deluxe, featuring a multipaged comic theme with scary pictures of demons coercing people to read versions other than the KJV.

We learned how to give these tracts to waitresses or those seated next to us on planes (especially if they looked fearful). If personal interaction made you uncomfortable, you could deposit these tracts stealthily in public restrooms, leave them in library books you were returning, or (one of my favorites) asking the toll booth attendant to give it to the person in the car behind you while you paid their toll. One pastor even showed me how to hold a tract next to your car and release it so that it would land at the feet of someone standing on the side of the road as you drove by at a cool 35 mph.

I wish I were kidding.

If someone trusted Christ during a gospel-tract presentation, we were suppose to say a number of things to the new convert, printed helpfully for us right on the back of the tract. We were to place an emphasis on Bible reading, prayer, and church attendance. We should also give them an assurance of their salvation, which usually sounded something like, *"Now, once you've trusted Christ, He promises never to leave or forsake you. Ever. John 10:29 tells us that those in Christ will never be removed from God's hand. So, from here on out, you are saved no matter what. Welcome to the family of God."*

What Does the Bible Say?

To be clear, I do believe the Bible teaches "once saved, always saved." Jesus was very clear on this:

> "All that the Father gives me will come to me, and whoever comes to me I will never cast out. . . . And this is the will of him who sent me, that I should lose nothing of all that he has given me." (John 6:37, 39 ESV)

Notice how many times words like *all* and *never* are used in that verse. *All* that the Father gives to Jesus come to Him; He turns away *none* and loses *none*. He raises *all* whom the Father gave to Him on that last day.

In another place, He said:

> "My sheep hear My voice, and I know them, and they
> follow Me. And I give them eternal life, and they shall never
> perish; neither shall anyone snatch them out of My hand."
> (John 10:27–28)

Jesus gives His sheep eternal life and they never perish, and not even the enemy, try as he may, can remove Jesus' children from His hand. Paul concurs:

> For whom He foreknew, He also predestined to be con-
> formed to the image of His Son. . . . Moreover whom He
> predestined, then He also called; whom He called, these He
> also justified; and whom He justified, these He also glorified.
> (Rom. 8:29–30)

There is no room for *any* to be lost in that progression. He doesn't say, "A large majority of those whom He predestined and called He also justified and glorified." *All* those He predestined He also glorified. Once God puts you on that train, the conductor makes sure you make it all the way to glory.

Those statements seem pretty straightforward.

Curiously, though, we *don't* find the apostles making statements to new believers like the ones I was making to my tract-converts after they had prayed to receive Jesus. In fact, they seem even to make our final salvation conditional on our continued obedience. For example, when Paul and Barnabas spoke to the new converts in Antioch, they didn't say, *"Now that you've trusted Christ, you will go to heaven, no matter what!"* Instead, they "persuaded them to continue in the grace of God" (Acts 13:43). In the next chapter Paul and Barnabas warned these same new converts to "continue in the faith," because only by persevering "through many tribulations" would they "enter the kingdom of God" (Acts 14:22).

Paul was concerned the new faith of his converts in Thessalonica would fade, making his initial work among them in vain:

> For this reason, when I could no longer endure it, I sent to know your faith, lest by some means the tempter had tempted you, and our labor might be in vain. (1 Thess. 3:5)

In other words, he lived with the fear that the "tempter" could take back all the ground he had gained through his initial preaching. He urged his converts not to waver from their confession of faith, stating that if they did, their initial response of faith would do them *no good*.

Similarly, to his Philippian converts, he said,

> You should hold fast to the word of life, so that I may rejoice in the day of Christ that I did not run in vain or labored in vain. (Phil. 2:16)

To the Romans, he said:

> Therefore consider the goodness and severity of God: on those who fell, severity; but toward you, goodness, if you continue in His goodness. Otherwise you also will be cut off. (Rom. 11:22)

Jude warned his young church:

> But you, beloved, building yourselves up on your most holy faith, praying in the Holy Spirit, *keep yourselves in the love of God*, looking for the mercy of our Lord Jesus Christ unto eternal life. (Jude 20–21, emphasis added)

The writer of Hebrews gave perhaps the strongest warnings:

> See to it that no one fails to obtain the grace of God; that no "root of bitterness" springs up and causes trouble, and by it many become defiled. (Heb. 12:15 ESV)

> Therefore we must give the more earnest heed to the things we have heard, lest we drift away. (Heb. 2:1)

This last verse depicts salvation as finding refuge from a terrible typhoon in a safe harbor. The writer urges his converts to "drop anchor" so that they don't "drift" back out into the typhoon of unbelief and judgment.

In another place, he warns:

> Beware, brethren, lest there be in any of you an evil heart of unbelief in departing from the living God; but exhort one another daily, while it is called "Today," lest any of you be hardened through the deceitfulness of sin. For we have become partakers in Christ *if we hold the beginning of our confidence steadfast to the end.* (Heb. 3:12–14, emphasis added)

Jesus warned:

> "If anyone does not abide in Me, he is cast out as a branch and is withered; and they gather them and throw them into the fire, and they are burned." (John 15:6)

> "Whoever denies Me before men, him I will also deny before My Father who is in heaven." (Matt. 10:33)

And He promised:

> "He who endures to the end will be saved." (Matt. 10:22)

> "To him who overcomes I will give to eat from the tree of life, which is in the midst of the Paradise of God." (Rev. 2:7)

> "He who overcomes shall not be hurt by the second death." (Rev. 2:11)

Clearly, only those who endure to the end will be saved. So, do these passages contradict the other passages that clearly teach, "once saved, always saved"?

Because the Bible is God's word, it cannot contradict itself.[1] In fact, many of the very authors issuing these warnings are the ones who also give us the glowing promises of eternal security.[2] *Surely the Bible writers are not so schizophrenic as to contradict themselves within the space of a few verses!*

These passages do not teach that you can lose your salvation. But they do teach you something important about the nature of saving faith: Saving faith always endures to the end.

These warnings ought to be taken at face value; however, if we fall away, we will not be saved in the end. But since those who are truly saved can never lose it, we must conclude that a failure to heed the warnings demonstrates that we never possessed *true* saving faith to begin with. How else could all these verses be true?[3]

> *Faith that fades, no matter how luscious its firstfruits, is not saving faith.*

Furthermore, I believe God gives the warnings *to believers* to solidify them in the faith. The warnings help us not take God's grace for granted. They sober us in moments of temptation and darkness. A true believer can never be lost, but a true believer also will never stop following Jesus. Those warnings spur me to keep following.

The Most Difficult Bible Passage

To demonstrate this, let's look at one of the most notoriously difficult passages in all of the New Testament:

> For it is impossible for those who were once enlightened, and have tasted the heavenly gift, and have become partakers of the Holy Spirit, and have tasted the good word of God and the powers of the age to come, if they fall away, to renew them again to repentance, since they crucify again for themselves the Son of God, and put Him to an open shame. (Heb. 6:4–6)

This passage is difficult on multiple levels. Not only does it sound like it is possible to "fall away," but that if you do so you can never come back! What are we to make of it?

A General Warning, Not an Individual Diagnosis

First, I think it's helpful to realize that the author is giving a general warning to a congregation, made up of both genuine and superficial believers, not diagnosing any one particular person's spiritual state. He is also not attempting to specify the mechanics of salvation.[4]

"Being enlightened" and "tasting of the age to come" and "partaking of the Holy Spirit" are more descriptions of the movement as a whole than they are certifications of any one particular person. Everyone who was part of that movement shared in these things, at least on some level.

In every congregation there are people who *get* caught up in the movement without experiencing true conversion. They get excited, learn the songs, pray the sinner's prayer, get baptized, and maybe even get involved in the mission, but these never translate into a deep, personal embrace of Jesus Christ. Over time, their enthusiasm fades.

What does he mean by "impossible to renew them to repentance"? The writer, bewildered by the failure of some of his readers to go all the way with Jesus, says, "If you have seen the glory of Jesus and been convinced of the truth of His resurrection, only to return intentionally to your sin, what else is left for me to say? What 'greater argument' is there left to use? What could possibly be more 'convincing' than Jesus' death and resurrection?" In other words, what's *left* to say that could move you to repentance?

In the verses that follow, he explains that hearing the gospel is like rain falling upon a piece of seeded farmland (6:7–8). If after being properly seeded and watered only thorns and thistles grow up, what else can you conclude but that the soil is worthless? In the same way, if hearing the gospel produces only the thorns of rebellion in your heart, what else can be done? The preaching of the gospel is God's source of resurrection life. If you are immune to it, there's no other tool God can wield.

Movements gain followers. Some become true believers; some simply get swept up in for the show and excitement. Only time will reveal the difference. This leads to a second observation.

The Faith that Saves Is the Faith that Endures to the End

This passage shows us that the only faith that saves is the faith that endures to the end. Many go through the initial motions of salvation, yet, after a period of time, fall back into their old ways. Such a person was never really saved to begin with, despite all their early, initial excitement.

Jesus once told a story about a farmer that planted seeds into various types of soil. One soil, He said, had a soft, top layer of dirt, and young saplings sprung up quickly. When the sun came out, however, these saplings dried up. Their roots did not go deep enough to withstand the heat of the sun.

> *These warnings ought to be taken at face value: if we fall away, we will not be saved in the end.*

Do these short-lived plants in Jesus' parable represent unsaved people or saved people? They represent unsaved people who *for a while* looked like they were saved people. These people, according to Jesus, "believe for a while and in time of temptation fall away" (Luke 8:13). Thought they had an encouraging beginning, one full of zeal and fervent devotion, in the end they withered and were cast out.

This shows us that the difference between saving faith and super-ficial faith has little to do the intensity of emotion at its beginning and everything to do with its duration over time. Faith that fades, no matter how luscious its firstfruits, is not saving faith.[5]

Praying a prayer to ask Jesus into your heart, even if it's followed by a flurry of emotion and religious fervor, is no proof that you are saved. Enduring in that faith to the end is.

The writer of Hebrews 6 urges us toward that kind of enduring faith. He says, "We desire that each one of you *show the same diligence* to the full assurance of hope until the end" (v. 11, emphasis added). We strive to persevere to show that we *are* saved. Assurance comes from con-tinuing to show the same diligence in faith you started with.

Those Who Fall Away Cannot Be Renewed Again to Repentance?

As to those who fall away not being able to be "renewed again to repentance"—well, it cannot mean that those who fall back into sinful habits after they are saved have forfeited their chance for salvation.

Even some of the greatest heroes in the Bible fell back into old sinful habits—sometimes really bad ones, and sometimes for long periods of time. It's called "backsliding," a church word meaning you "slide back" into old sinful habits.

One of Paul's travelling companions, a guy named John Mark, abandoned the mission field because it got difficult, only to be restored later. Think about that—he *abandoned* the apostle Paul. He "put his hand to the plow and looked back," thus showing he was not fit for the kingdom of God.[6] Yet he was later restored to full usefulness in the king-dom (Acts 13:5, 13; 2 Tim. 4:11).

Abraham, whom the writer uses in this chapter (Heb. 6) as an example of persevering faith (6:15), doubted God so severely that he told another man his wife was his sister and that he could sleep with her—just to save himself![7] That's more than just a moral lapse; that's dirtbag behavior. He too was a "saved" man, brought back later to repentance, restoration, and great usefulness for the kingdom of God.

In 1 Corinthians Paul even describes a church member sleeping with his mother, whom he calls on the church to discipline (that is, put outside of its fellowship and treat like an unbeliever). The *purpose* of that discipline, however, was *to restore his soul to God* (1 Cor. 5:1–5). This guy's sin was not just a "mistake" or a "moral indiscretion." Sleeping with your mom doesn't get you put on a church prayer list; it gets you on the Jerry Springer show. Yet Paul believed he could be brought back.

Jesus said that no one who came to Him He would ever, for any reason, cast out.[8] *Ever.* If you are willing to repent, He will always receive you.

So what, then, does the writer mean when he says it is "impossible" to renew those who have fallen away to repentance?

Well, as we've already seen, His saying that if you've hardened your heart to the cross, there's nothing left to say to you, no "better" weapon in God's arsenal.

Furthermore, Scripture speaks of so hardening your heart against God's spirit he leaves you alone. God said in Genesis, "My Spirit shall not strive with man forever" (6:3). In the Gospel of Luke Jesus refers to this as the blasphemy against the Holy Spirit, a sin for which there is no forgiveness.[9] Many of those the writer is addressing are in danger of committing this kind of sin against the Spirit.

One caveat—I know many who fear they have committed this blasphemy and thus forfeited their opportunity to be saved. I thought that for a while. I thought that I had seen so much when I turned away and sinned so egregiously in the face of God's great kindnesses to me that surely I had blasphemed the Spirit.

I don't have space to unpack all the passages about blasphemy against the Spirit here (others have done so very thoroughly elsewhere)[10] but, as the popular advice goes, if you are worried that you have committed that blasphemy, you probably haven't. The final falling away to which Jesus and the writer of Hebrews refers includes the removal of any desire to be reconciled to Jesus. To say, they "can't be renewed to repentance," means they don't want to repent. Wanting to repent is the sign God hasn't abandoned you. It is God, after all, who puts in us the desire to come to Him.[11] Thus, your fear about having reached the point of no return is good proof that you haven't. If you want to repent, He will always receive you. He will not cast out, for any reason, any who come to Him.[12] "Whosoever will" can always come.

> *What we do know is that the Bible is full of stories of God saving people who looked to everyone else like they were beyond all hope.*

Furthermore, we should never give up on someone for whom we are praying on the basis that "the Spirit of God is no longer striving with them." If and when that happens to a person, we cannot know it. What we *do know* is that the Bible is full of stories of God saving people who looked to everyone else like they were beyond all hope. The *purpose* of these warnings is not to help us diagnose stubborn people so that we *stop* praying for them, but to feel the urgency of the situation so that we *start* doing so more persistently. The only time we can conclude that God's Spirit is no longer striving with someone is when they are dead. Until then, we have the responsibility to pray and they have the opportunity to repent.

Perhaps there is someone reading this who has not yet come to Christ. These warnings make you think, *This must be what has happened to me. I have "fallen away after being enlightened."* I must have committed the blasphemy against the Holy Spirit. It is impossible for me now to repent." Or you see the writer's analogy about the rain producing only thorns and thistles and you think, *That's me! I heard the gospel and did not repent. Is my heart fatally flawed? Am I "un-savable"?*

For a while my wife thought she couldn't repent because she was not "predestined" by God for salvation. The gospel she had heard so many times growing up had failed to take root in her heart and so she concluded that something was fundamentally wrong with her heart. When she graduated from high school, she concluded that she might as well pursue a life of sin because there was nothing she could do to reverse God's decrees.

The Bible *never* tells us, however, to analyze the wickedness of our or anyone's hearts or to speculate about God's electing providence. It simply commands us to repent. "If you hear God's voice," the writer of Hebrews says, "obey today." That means the choice right now is yours. In Matthew 23:37 Jesus said, "O Jerusalem, Jerusalem . . . how often would I have gathered your children together . . . (but) *you* would not." Jesus did not say, ". . . but I didn't elect you," He said, "But you wouldn't come."

You need wait on nothing else from God. You have the opportunity and obligation, right now, to repent. If you obey that command, God will save you.[13]

The gospel message is that there was something fundamentally wrong with my wife's heart: it was spiritually dead. The good news of the gospel is that God makes dead hearts alive.[14] God turns hearts of stone into hearts of flesh. He transformed Saul, a Pharisaical, Jesus-hating murderer, enemy #1 of the early church, into Paul, its greatest spokesman and advocate. He can do that for you, too. You just have to ask Him.

So don't turn what the writer intended to be an encouragement to repent into a discouragement from it. He is not trying to help you determine your election status. He is trying to communicate the seriousness of the gospel you've heard and to urge you to obey it today.

Assured of Better Things—Things that Belong to Salvation

Despite the warnings he gives about the dangers of falling away, the writer of Hebrews says, "But, beloved, we are confident of better things concerning you, yes, things that accompany salvation" (6:9). He sees so much evidence of true salvation in their lives—a love for God's name and a love for God's people, for example—that he is convinced they will not fall away. Saving faith does not fade, and the writer is convinced (by their dramatic change of life and current spiritual fruits) that they possess such faith.

He is confident that "He who has begun a good work in you will complete it until the day of Jesus Christ" (Phil. 1:6). He encourages them to see the clear evidences of God's grace at work in their lives and place their hope in the God who started the whole process. What God started in them He surely will finish.

How do you know you will endure to the end? Well, do you see strong evidence of grace in you right now, "things that accompany salvation"? That is an additional assurance you are saved. More on that in the next chapter.

The "Real" Doctrine of Eternal Security

It's not incorrect to say "once saved, always saved." It's just incomplete. The full doctrine of "eternal security" is that once we are saved, we will always be saved, *and* that those who are saved will persevere in their faith to the end. It is true that "once saved, always saved"; but it is also true that *"once saved, forever following."*

As I noted at the beginning of this chapter, a perversion of the doctrine of eternal security has become common in evangelical circles. This perversion presents salvation as a contract "signed" with God that God can never get out of, no matter what you do. Once you've signed the contract and prayed the prayer, you've got God trapped.

> *It's not incorrect to say "once saved, always saved." It's just incomplete.*

Scripture does not present salvation that way. Salvation is a posture of repentance and faith toward Christ that you adopt at your conversion and maintain for a lifetime. If you permanently abandon that posture later in life, your faith was likely not saving faith.

Shortly after college I read John Bunyan's classic *Pilgrim's Progress* and realized that Bunyan's presentation of eternal security was different than the way I had always heard it explained. Bunyan's (who was a Baptist and believed in eternal security) protagonist in *Pilgrim's Progress*, Christian, encounters many people on his path

> *"Faith that fizzles before the finish was flawed from the first."*

to the Celestial City who had begun on the path toward heaven only to depart it when the going got tough. These people, in Bunyan's view, were never saved, despite their initial confession and beginning steps of faith. Bunyan's message was clear: those who do not persevere until the end are not saved and will not end up in heaven.

Wayne Grudem concludes: *"The perseverance of the saints means that all those who are truly born again will be kept by God's power and will persevere as Christians until the end of their lives, and that only those who persevere until the end have been truly born again."*[15]

Or, in a slightly less academic form, "Faith that fizzles before the finish was flawed from the first."

Making Our "Calling and Election" Sure

So—Hebrews 6:4–6 shows us that true believers cannot lose their salvation, but one of the evidences that we have saving belief is that it endures to the end.

The warnings against falling away are given, however, not only to reveal that people who don't persevere to the end aren't truly saved, but also to spur true believers to continue on in the faith. We are warned that if we fall into sin and stay there that we will not be saved. So these warnings compel us to get back up and stay in the faith, thus proving we are saved.

> *It is true that "once saved, always saved"; but it is also true that "once saved, forever following."*

In other words, we are not to take a "wait and see" posture about whether or not we have truly been saved: *"Well, I'm falling away right now, that must mean I am not saved."* Instead, we are commanded to *labor* and to *strive* to keep ourselves in the faith. Peter tells us to be eager to "make our calling and election" sure.[16] We are to "work out" our salvation with fear and trembling.[17] By persevering in the faith, we prove we have been born again. When we fall, these warnings compel us to get back up again.

Heeding the warnings shows that we possess the salvation that we can never lose. Failing to heed the warnings shows that we never had it to begin with.

Make your mind feel like it is going to explode? Then you're probably getting it.

The writer of Hebrews 6 tells us to persevere to the end so that we can have "the full assurance of hope." As we persevere to the end, we *maintain* that full assurance of hope. Persevering in the faith continually reassures us of our salvation.

As we saw in chapter 4, conversion is a posture of repentance and faith that we begin at a moment but maintain for a lifetime. The best proof that we were saved in the past is our posture in the present.

Thus, our perseverance in holy living is not the basis of our salvation, but it is a source of our assurance. The Reformed tradition says it this way: by following God's commands we *"maintain the assurance of [our] perseverance."*[18]

So, like repentance and faith, *perseverance* and *assurance of salvation* are two sides of the same coin. One can never be possessed apart from the other. So, if you want to know for sure that you are saved, maintain your posture of repentance toward God and faith in Christ. Persevering in the faith is *how* we make our calling and election sure.

How Do You Know Whether You Are "Backslidden" or Not Truly Saved?

Every Christian "backslides"—technically, any time you sin you are backsliding. I do it dozens of times each day. That doesn't mean I'm not saved.

How long can you backslide before you conclude your initial profession of faith wasn't real? Six months? Five years? Twenty years?

There's no real clear answer on this because the Bible never specifies a time limit. As I mentioned before, some Bible heroes (like David, Peter, and others) fell back into sin for a long time before God brought them back. There are others, however, of whom the apostle John says, "They went out from us, but they were not of us" (1 John 2:19). The reason they did not persist in the faith was they were never saved to begin with. They were the seeds Jesus spoke of that sprang up quickly and faded away.

So if a professing believer falls into sin and then comes back, how can you tell if he was a genuine believer who simply backslid or a superficial believer who wasn't truly converted?

Tough question.

For some people, the life change at their conversion was so significant and their lapse into sin was so brief that it seems obvious that their conversion took place in the past and their fall back into sin was just a brief lapse.

For others, the opposite is true—because there was hardly any life change after their initial profession of faith and the gospel really seemed to come alive to them at some later point, it makes sense to think of that later experience as their true conversion. We see this happen all the time at our church. Someone says, "I asked Jesus into my heart when I was a kid and I even got baptized . . . but I feel like for the first time I'm understanding the gospel." Their faith, for the first time, becomes real. It is obvious that this was their real point of conversion.

For many, however, the answer is not as obvious either way. You're not sure if your "re-awakening to the gospel" was simply repentance from a time of backsliding or your true conversion. So what do you do?

At the end of the day, knowing the moment of your conversion is not essential. What is essential is to know that you are currently in a posture of repentance and faith. Regardless of when you first assumed the posture, the fact that you are in it now assures you of your salvation. Knowing *when* it first happened may be helpful; knowing *that* you are trusting in Him now is essential.

As a believer, you will struggle with indwelling sin for the rest of your life. The greatest saints have experienced such bitter, unsuccessful struggles with sin that it almost drove them to despair! Like the hymn writer, you'll probably want to exclaim,

> *Prone to wander, Lord I feel it;*
> *Prone to leave the God I love;*
> *Here's my heart, Lord, take and seal it,*
> *Seal it for Thy courts above!*[19]

That kind of heartfelt prayer is really good proof of saving faith. The struggle should assure us of salvation, not make us doubt it.

As Tom Schreiner says it, "Perseverance is not perfection; it is a new direction."[20] You may sometimes fall, but each time you get up again, looking heavenward. "The righteous man falls seven times and gets back up again." The trajectory of your life is a cry for God to change your heart, even as sometimes you stumble and fall. Your healing may be gradual, but it is happening.

Which Are More Important—the Assurances or the Warnings?

As a Bible teacher, I know that when I emphasize the warnings about falling away some genuinely saved people will be shaken in their faith. I also know that if I don't emphasize the warnings, some people who aren't saved will die lost thinking they are OK because they prayed a prayer. Both emphasizing and not-emphasizing the warnings have collateral damage.

The Bible gives both assurances and warnings, and so should we. The Holy Spirit tells us, "Examine yourselves as to whether you are [really] in the faith" (2 Cor. 13:5). But He also assures us that we belong to Jesus, we are safe in His hand, and that when we are faithless, He'll remain faithful.[21]

I have sympathy for people on both sides of the issue. For a while I was a falsely-assured impostor, and I'm glad a Sunday school teacher helped me see that my superficial confession of faith would not save me on the day of judgment. God used his warning to rouse me out of my slumber.

But I also know the struggle of being unable to find assurance after my salvation. Doubting made my life miserable.

God gives both warnings and assurances because both are *necessary for Christian growth*. Both solidify us in the faith that saves.

If you want to teach the Bible well, emphasize both, and in the same proportions the Bible emphasizes them. Trust that the Holy Spirit will use both for the purposes He intended.

God gives both warnings and assurances because both are necessary for Christian growth.

Sometimes a word of warning will rattle someone who is truly saved. Sometimes words of assurance will give false hope to an unbeliever. But as you give proper weight and attention to both, trust that those who stick around to listen long enough will find the full assurance of faith God desires them to have.

The Full Assurance of Hope

God warns us about the dangers of falling away because He wants to rouse the falsely assured out of their slumber before it is eternally too late.

He also wants to compel believers onward to the finish line. Perseverance in the faith assures us we are saved.

There are other ways, however, that we can verify God's grace at work in us. The book of 1 John gives several confirmatory "tests" that show the Spirit is at work in our hearts. These "evidences of grace" are what made the writer of Hebrews "feel sure of better things—things that belong to salvation" for his readers (Heb. 6:9). Seeing these evidences of God's work in us help us gain confidence that "He who has begun a good work in [us] will complete it until the day of Jesus Christ" (Phil. 1:6). They help us know we will persevere because we see the evidence of God's work in us, and we know that what He started, He will finish.

To these "tests" we will now turn.

THE EVIDENCE YOU
HAVE BELIEVED

In college, one of my best friends lived in a house off campus. Now, college guys, in general, are not usually what you would call "clean," but this guy took domestic filth to a whole new level. He and his roommates rarely did their dishes. And by "rarely" I mean "never." Plates covered with decaying food and radioactive biotic samples piled up in the sink. Each morning my best friend left his old cereal bowl, filled with milk, on the breakfast table. And don't get me started on their bathroom. . . . Put it this way, if we had still been living in Old Testament days, going into their bathroom would have defiled you and your offspring for four generations. Furthermore, they had a cat that did not get the "litter box" concept. When you walked into their house, you were greeted by a concoction of odors that eye has not seen, nor has ear heard, nor has entered into the heart of man.

Twice a semester, my best friend's mother came to visit. She would usually arrive on a Friday, and her first order of business was to cleanse the house, which usually involved a blowtorch and napalm. For the first few days after she had visited, the house smelled not like mildew and toxic rot, but lemons and Ajax.

That smell was the infallible indicator of her presence. Had I walked into their house one Sunday and been greeted by the usual cocktail of foul fragrances, and then been told by my friend that his mother had come earlier that week, I would have said, "You're lying. Had your mother been here, this place would smell different."

The Proof of His Presence

This is essentially what the apostle John concludes about the presence of Jesus in a believer's life:

> He who believes in the Son of God has the witness *in himself*. . . . He who has the Son has life; he who does not have the Son of God does not have life. (1 John 5:10, 12, emphasis added)

Recall that "life" for John does not simply refer to living eternally after we die, but possessing the life of God in us now. In the previous five chapters, John lays out these evidences. For example:

> Now by this we know that we know Him, if we *keep His commandments*. He who says, "I know Him," and does not keep His commandments, is a liar, and the truth is not in him. But whoever keeps His word, truly the love of God is perfected in him. By this we know that we are in Him. He who says he abides in Him ought himself also to *walk just as He walked*. (1 John 2:3–6, emphasis added)

> He who says he is in the light, and hates his brother, is in darkness until now. (1 John 2:9)

> If anyone loves the world, the love of the Father is not in him. (1 John 2:15)

> If you know that He is righteous, you know that *every-one who practices righteousness* is born of Him. (1 John 2:29, emphasis added)

> No one who abides in him keeps on sinning; no one who keeps on sinning has either seen him or known him. (1 John 3:6 ESV)

Saving faith proves itself not only by persevering to the end, but by certain inexorable changes it makes in the heart. The presence of these new affections helps assure us that God's grace has gone to work within us. The writer of Hebrews had seen these evidences of grace in the lives of his readers, which is why he was "assured" that they would persevere to the end—he saw in them "things that belong to salvation," so he was assured of "better things" for them than falling away (Heb. 6:9). These changes demonstrate that Jesus' eternal life has gone to work within you, and as you see them you can be confident that He who has begun a good work in you will bring it to completion (Phil. 1:6)

I think you can boil down John's list of "heart changes" into essentially two categories:

A Love for God

The new, living heart is characterized by a love for God. Correspondingly, sin begins to take on a certain hollowness, even dreadfulness.

As a pastor, I've watched this process happen numerous times in the lives of new believers. Whereas the word of God once seemed boring and burdensome, it becomes captivating and thrilling. The goodness and majesty of God explode in their hearts. Time and time again, I've seen people wake up from the daze of worldliness and see the superior glory of the gospel.

Here's a letter I received recently from someone at our church going through such a process, coinciding with a family tragedy. They had known about the "love of Jesus" for years, but it had never gripped their hearts.

> My wife blamed herself and we cried daily as we left the hospital with no baby. In our moment of distress my wife leaned over to me and said, "Jesus still loves us even in our pain." She found an internal peace in Christ and it was amazing. I later heard Christ whisper in my ears, "Jesus died for you, and even if you walk away from this hospital without your son, Christ is enough." It was in that moment that the gospel awakened in me.

The sense of the glory of God they had known in their minds awakened in their hearts. It produced in them, for the first time, a deep, personal love for the Father. *This is the sign that God has gone to work.* You begin to love God like a Father. Your spirit begins to cry out "Abba (Daddy)" (Rom. 8:15).

When you have been born again, you begin to avoid sin not just because you fear punishment, but because it keeps you from God. You begin to seek God because you love God; you begin to do righteousness because you crave righteousness. Your spiritual tastes have changed.

When I lived in Southeast Asia, I was introduced to a fruit called "durian." The locals loved it. The opening of durian season was like a national holiday. People got off work to get to the market and buy a bushel-load for their families. The problem is that it smells like a mixture of Cap'n Crunch and armpit. I would get nauseous even being around it. I couldn't imagine putting it in my mouth.

After I had been there for a year, I noticed that it quit smelling so badly. Eventually, I got to where I could eat it. And then I found myself enjoying it in small quantities. Then large ones. Then craving it. Now, I can say it is one of my favorite fruits, and one of the things I miss most from living there. I'm still not a huge fan of Cap'n Crunch and armpit, but I love durian.

Whereas you once would have had to force me to eat it, I now eat it freely—even eagerly. The fruit didn't change; my tastes did. Likewise, the Spirit of God transforms our spiritual tastes, so that the gospel that was once foolish and offensive to us becomes sweet and savory.[1] Paul said the "fragrance of Christ" is to those who are perishing like the rotten smell of death, but to those being saved like the sweet aroma of life.[2] The same gospel; different spiritual appetites.

Once God has given you an appetite for Him, you won't need to be forced to seek Him. You couldn't be stopped from seeking Him. Your obedience is less about duty and more about delight.

> *Once God has given you an appetite for Him, you won't need to be forced to seek Him.*

Christians do not cease to pursue sin because they have developed wills of iron; they cease sinning because they have been given a new nature which loves what God loves.[3]

Again, don't think this happens all at once. Like Paul, our flesh and our regenerated spirit will struggle against one another for the rest of our lives. The evidence that God has worked in your heart, though, is the presence of a growing desire for God, a heart that "delights" in its innermost being in the law of God even while our flesh craves sin.[4]

A Love for Others

Another sign you have been born again, the apostle John says, is that you start to love others, particularly believers:

> We know that we have passed from death to life, because we love the brethren. He who does not love his brother abides in death. Whoever hates his brother is a murderer, and you know that no murderer has eternal life abiding in him. By this we know love, because He laid down His life for us. And we also ought to lay down our lives for the brethren. (1 John 3:14–16)

No one can experience the love of Christ for them and not overflow with it toward others, especially those who share our love for Jesus and experience of His grace. Scripture goes so far as to say that loving others is *the* sign that you really understand the gospel.

In Matthew 18:23–35, Jesus describes a man who owed another man an extraordinary amount of money—"ten thousand talents."[5] The day came when the debt was due, and the man was called in to see his loan officer. Of course, the man couldn't pay.

In those days, when you couldn't pay a debt, you were sent to a "debtor's prison" where you endured hard labor until your account was settled. If you died in prison before you paid off the debt, your children became responsible for it. Then their children. This is how whole families became enslaved to other ones.

This man's debt was so large that it had ensured his family's imprisonment for generations to come. On that day of reckoning, the debt-consumed man threw himself in desperation upon the mercy of the loaner—he needed more time to pay off the debt. Loan officers, of course, aren't known for being "merciful." They don't get to be where they are by having a soft spot. Even today we don't call them "loan bunnies" or "loan puppies," we call them "loan sharks." If you don't pay what you owe, they send someone named Bruno to your house to break your thumbs.

Everyone in this courtroom watching this pathetic scene unfold no doubt felt uncomfortable, as they knew judgment was about to fall on the head of this man. But then the most unexpected thing happened. The loan shark feels what Jesus called *splagma*, a Greek word meaning a deep, groaning compassion. We don't know why. Maybe he was reminded of his own son, or maybe he saw in him a picture of himself. He got teary-eyed. His bottom lip started to quiver. Then he said something no one was expecting: "I won't just give you 'more time.' I am wiping out your debt entirely. You owe me nothing more. Go—you are free."

No one in the courtroom could believe it, least of all the forgiven man. When he finally convinced himself this wasn't a joke, he stood up and, for the first time in as long as he could remember the weight of the world was gone off of his shoulders. He thanked the loan officer profusely and ran out of the courtroom a new man, rushing home to tell his family the news of his (and their) release.

As he crossed the street across from the courthouse, however, he saw an old colleague who owed him $10 he had borrowed for groceries a month before. He shouted out to the man, "Hey, do you have that $10 you owe me?" The man replied, "I'm sorry; it's been a rough week. I have no cash. I'll pay you next week. I promise."

The forgiven man flew into a rage and screamed, "No! Time is up! If you can't pay me my $10 right now, I'm throwing you into prison."

At this point in the story, Jesus' audience would have rolled their eyes in disbelief. "No way. There is no way a man forgiven of ten thousand talents could hold another guy responsible for $10."

And that was Jesus' point exactly. Anyone who has the slightest grasp on how much grace God has shown to them in salvation can hardly be ungracious toward others. When you understand how much you've been forgiven, you will forgive.

Jesus concludes His story in a sobering, if not downright alarming, way. The original loan officer, hearing of the man's ungratefulness, hauled the man back into court. "And in anger [he] delivered him to the jailors, until he should pay all the debt" (Matt. 18:34 ESV). The man in Jesus' story was lost forever.

Did Jesus mean that Christians who fail to forgive lose their salvation? No. He meant that if we are not of a generous spirit we likely have never been saved, or so lost touch with it we can hardly be said to understand it any longer. Like the Hebrews writer explained, they have "tasted" of the heavenly gift but never really swallowed it.

Those people who have experienced the gospel show it by becoming like the gospel. On that final day, if we have given to others only what they deserved, God likely will be giving to us what we deserve. Though we sat through a lot of sermons and memorized a lot of verses, we never encountered the grace of the gospel.

The sign that you have experienced grace is that you become gracious. Patience, forgiveness, generosity, delight in and compassion toward others are inevitable fruits of the gospel root. So,

> *If you are selfish with your possessions, how could you really have experienced the generosity of the gospel?*

> *If you are unmoved by the plight of the outcast, how could you have experienced the reconciliation of the gospel?*

> *If your only ambition in life is to grow rich, famous, and obtain all of your dreams, is there any possible way you have understood what it cost Jesus to obtain your salvation?*

If the gospel has taken root inside of you, when others make fun of the outcast, you can't, because somewhere inside of you, you realize that you were the outcast when Jesus came for you (Heb. 13:12–13). When you think about what you want to do with your life, your career, and your material possessions, you *can't* think simply of how to leverage them for self-promotion. Jesus, who was rich and famous, left what He had to bless you (2 Cor. 8:9). You want to know how you can do the same for others.

This is the apostle John's point in his first letter. If Jesus Christ is really *in* you, then you will show evidences of that by loving what, and whom, He loves and seeking whom and what He seeks.

I once had a friend whose six-year-old daughter approached him about "accepting Jesus." Because he didn't know any other way of explaining it, he led her in a prayer in which she asked Jesus into her heart. About a week later she came to him and said, "Dad, how big was Jesus?" He said, "I don't know. He was a grown man, but people were shorter back then. Maybe about 5' 10"?"

"Daddy, how tall am I?"

"About 3' 6"."

"Daddy, I'm confused. If Jesus was 5' 10" and I am 3' 6", and Jesus came into my heart, shouldn't He just kind of poke out everywhere?"

There is some profound truth in what my friend's daughter said. If the Jesus of eternal life has come to dwell in you, the evidence of that eternal life will overshadow you.

"But I Still Love Sin!"

At this point, you might again be tempted to despair, because if you have even the slightest self-awareness you probably recognize strong undercurrents of selfishness, idolatry, apathy, and unbelief still present in your heart. Does that mean you are not genuinely saved?

That's not what you should necessarily conclude. As we've seen, the apostles all testify to a never-ending and intense struggle they had with sin.[6] James says that we sin (even as believers) because we are "drawn away by [our] own desires and enticed" (James 1:14). I assume he says that from experience. I find my own heart prone to unforgiveness, resentment, jealousy, and selfishness more often than I care to admit.

So hear this clearly: *Believers can and do struggle with just about any kind of sinful lust.* Martin Luther said that in the gospel was we were *simul iustus et peccator,* or "simultaneously declared righteous while yet still sinners." Even after we have been saved our sinful flesh craves unrighteousness.

In fact, the presence of the struggle itself can be affirmation that God's Spirit is at work within you. Before God's Spirit came into you, you didn't struggle against sin—you ran toward it eagerly! An unbeliever might "struggle" with sin, but typically they are struggling only with its unwanted consequences or the feelings of guilt and shame that accompany it. A believer's struggle is much deeper. Their struggle is with the wickedness of the sin itself and the grievousness of its offense to God. When God's Spirit lives in you, you feel the tension of that struggle every day. The struggle is not an indication that you're not saved; it is, in fact, the evidence that you *are.*

The more I have grown in Christ, *the more* (not less) I've felt my sinfulness. The more God's light has illuminated my heart, the more I've been able to see how messed up I really am. In fact, I seem *more* sinful to myself now than I did in the days when I first came to know Christ! The light of God's grace first came into my heart like a small, flickering flame that allowed me to see the "big" problems in it. Now that flame has turned into a lantern, I can see smaller things. As the light grows brighter, I even see the "dust" of sin layering all that I say and do. Indeed, if we could see our heart as God does, we'd see that there is nothing we do that is not tainted by sin. Even our most righteous acts are tainted with impurity.

Often the strongest evidence of my growth in grace is my growth in the knowledge of my need for grace.[7]

It Takes a Village to Identify Regeneration

Identifying the evidences of true regeneration if your life can be difficult, if not impossible, to do on your own. Some are prone to discouragement and self-condemnation, others to an overly optimistic view of themselves. God gave us the local church to help us see ourselves accurately. Mike McKinley, in his fantastic little book on assurance, *Am I Really a Christian*, says:

> I can't stress enough that this important process of examination can only be properly done in the context of a local church. You need other Christians who are committed to your spiritual well-being. They are the ones who will be able to get to know you and identify the fruit of the new birth in your life. . . . We are not good judges of our own hearts. Some people are entirely too easy on themselves. They imagine that they give evidence of genuine regret and repentance for their sin when in reality there is none. Others with a tender conscience are far too hard on themselves. They take every weakness and failure as evidence that they are hypocrites and false Christians. Being involved in a local church is immensely helpful for both kinds of people.[8]

So far we have identified three primary bases for assurance: a present posture of faith and repentance; perseverance in the faith; and evidences of eternal life in our heart—a love for God and a love for others, particularly other believers. These three combine to give us a powerful sense of assurance that we belong to God.

Still, there are moments—moments where your attraction to the lusts of the flesh, or the weakness of your desire for God, or the degree of selfishness toward your children, make you wonder whether or not you're really saved. *Where do you turn in those moments of despair?* That will be the subject of our final chapter.

WHEN YOU CONTINUE TO DOUBT

There are times, even now, when I look at my heart and wonder how I could possibly have been "born again." Moments in which I care more about what's coming on TV that night than I do the spread of the gospel in the world. Moments when God feels distant, almost like a stranger. My emotions for Him are lukewarm, if not downright cold. I don't jump out of bed hungry for His Word, and my mind wanders all over the place when I pray. Or I fall to that same old temptation again. For the thousandth time. Or moments I doubt God's goodness, even His existence.

It's not how I feel all the time, or even most of the time, but it is how I feel some of the time.

And then the question hits me again: *Wait a minute . . . Am I **really** saved? How could I be, and still have feelings like this?*

What do you do in that moment? Pray "the sinners' prayer" again? Should I call my old church and have the pastor warm up the baptismal waters?

The answer is relatively simple in that moment: *keep believing the gospel.* Keep your hand on the head of the Lord Jesus Christ. No matter how you feel at any given moment, how encouraged or discouraged you feel about your spiritual progress, how hot or cold your love for Jesus, what you should be doing is always the same—resting in the gospel. Rest in His finished work. That's all you can do. It's all you need to do. It's all God has commanded you to do.

> *On your very best of days, you must rest all your hopes on God's grace. On your worst of days, He should be your refuge and hope.*

On your very best of days, you must rest all your hopes on God's grace. On your worst of days, His finished work should be your refuge. Your posture should always be one of dependence on His finished work and hope in His indwelling Spirit. Period.

Diagnosis Is Not the Same as Prescription

A medical diagnosis tells you what is wrong; a prescription tells you what to do about it. God's prescription for every diagnosed spiritual malady is faith in the gospel. Faith in the gospel imputes righteousness for the believer and releases Spirit-life in the soul.[1] "The law" diagnoses our problem; faith in the gospel provides the solution.

The Bible time and time again reminds us that no one is immune from doubt, spiritual apathy, and severe temptation. Elijah sank into self-pity and depression right after his stunning victory on Mt. Carmel. After speaking with God face-to-face, Moses lost his temper and blasphemed God publicly. After establishing the greatest kingdom Israel had ever seen, David committed adultery and murder. After preaching a sermon in which three thousand people were saved, Peter fell back into hypocrisy and cowardice. Perhaps God lets his saints struggle that way so that their faith will remain in his grace and not in their righteousness.

Pride, C. S. Lewis said, is the worst of all the sins. It is the one sin God says, "He resists," and it fuels all the other sins. God therefore allows us to struggle with lesser sins to keep us from that greatest of sins.[2]

In that light, see your ongoing struggle with sin as God's invitation to rest humbly in the gospel; to declare again that Christ's cross is your only hope. In your moment of weakness and doubt, re-believe the gospel. Renew your posture of submission toward Him and rest in the news of His finished work. "To progress," Martin Luther said, "is always to begin again."

And here is the good news: in the unlikely chance that your lack of spiritual progress really was the result of not being born again, the moment you rest in the gospel you will be. In other words, if what you think is "renewed" faith in the gospel turns out to be "first" faith, you will still be saved in the end. Even if you can't pinpoint the moment your salvation happened in the past, at least you know you are in the present. You are resting in Christ, which is what God wanted from you all along.

> *"To progress is always to begin again."*

I'm not saying that you should think of yourself as getting re-saved every other moment, or that there is no way to be sure you were saved yesterday or the day before. I'm simply saying that whenever you doubt your standing with God, the solution is the same: trust in the finished work of Jesus.

"But I Don't Feel Saved."

Perhaps sometimes you don't *feel* saved, or *feel* that close to God. What should you do then? Feelings are fickle and dangerously misleading, and Scripture *never* points us to our "feelings" for assurance. Our assurance ought to be based on the fact of Christ's finished work; our "feelings of assurance" will come from maintaining faith in that finished work. In other words, feelings come *from* assurance, not assurance from feelings.

In high school my father gave me a marvelous little word-picture of this: Imagine, he said, three men walking in a line along the top of a narrow city wall. The first in line is named "Fact"; the second, "Faith"; the third, "Feeling." Because the wall is narrow, they need to pay careful attention to where they step. As long as "Feeling's" eyes are on "Faith," and "Faith's" eyes are on "Fact," they will all do fine. But the moment that "Faith" takes its eyes off of "Fact" and turns around to check on "Feeling," both "Faith" and "Feeling" will fall off the wall.

Our feelings can quickly deceive us—a weakness our Enemy loves to exploit. He loves to approach us in the midst of a temptation, or in a time of spiritual defeat or depression, and tell us that if we really belonged to Jesus we would not feel this way. He tries to use our *feelings* to get us to doubt our *faith.* "Feelings," however, are the fruit of faith. They should never be its source. Around our church we say, *"Don't feel your way into your beliefs; believe your way into your feelings."*

> *Don't feel your way into your beliefs; believe your way into your feelings.*

John Bunyan, the author of *Pilgrim's Progress,* described how assurance came to him only as he beheld the fact of Christ seated beside the Father, signifying that the work of Bunyan's salvation was completed. Prior to this, he said, his assurance would go "in and out" continually, up to twenty times a day! One moment, sure he was saved; the next, wondering if he'd felt sorry enough for his sin or had robust enough a faith to be born again. But one day, he said, as I was passing through a field, suddenly I thought of a sentence from the Scripture, and that sentence was, "Your righteousness is in heaven," and with the eyes of faith I saw Christ sitting at God's right hand, and suddenly I realized, there is my righteousness, and wherever I was, or whatever I was a-doing, God could never say to me, "Your righteousness is insufficient," for it was always before Him. I saw that my good frame of heart could not make my righteousness better, nor a bad frame make my righteousness worse; for my righteousness was Jesus Christ Himself, the same yesterday, and today, and forever.

And now did my chains fall off indeed. I was loosed from my afflictions and my irons; my doubts fled away . . . now I also went home rejoicing for the grace and love of God.[3]

Because Jesus' position before the Father is secure, our position with the Father is secure as well. Resting in that *fact* produces the feelings of assurance.

Where We've Come

In this book I have tried to show that God wants us to know that we are secure with Him, just as we want our beloved to know they are secure with us. That assurance is not found by remembering a prayer that you prayed, however, but by continuing in the posture of repentance and faith that you began at your conversion.

Jesus said that those who repent and believe will be saved. Repentance and faith are postures you begin in a moment but maintain for a lifetime. Those who persist in that posture can be assured that they are saved, and their lives will bear spiritual fruits that further prove their regeneration.

My purpose in this book hasn't been to rail against the sinner's prayer. I have led many to pray that prayer as an expression of their faith and, hopefully, will lead many more to do so. My purpose is to get at the basis of assurance. Because of my own experience with asking Jesus into my heart thousands of times, and still not being able to find peace, and because of a growing concern with people who think they're going to heaven simply because they've prayed a prayer, I want to be clear that what saves the sinner is a posture of repentance and faith toward Christ, that and that alone. Any "sinner's prayer" is only good insofar as it expresses that posture.

Christ finished the work of your salvation two thousand years ago. Rest in the fact of His finished work, and your feelings of assurance will grow. And so will all the other spiritual fruits.

When you feel like your heart is so bad that you could not possibly be born again, rejoice in the fact that you have been crucified in Christ and He has put your sin away forever. When you fear that you will be one to whom Christ says, "Depart from Me, I never knew you," rest in His promise to receive all who hope in His finished work. Charles Spurgeon, reflecting on those whom Christ turns away in Matthew 7:21–23, said (and I paraphrase), "Never knew *me*, Lord? How could You say that? When I had no hope of salvation, I rested all my hope on You. When I despaired in my struggle against sin, I looked to You for strength. Jesus could never say to me, 'I never knew you!'" [4]

None who lean the weight of their soul on the truth of the testimony God gave about Jesus as their hope of salvation will ever hear the words, "Depart from Me, I never knew you." To rest in Christ's finished work, you see, is to be known by Jesus.

I don't want to close the door on the possibility, however, that the reason you doubt your salvation is because you have never really come to know Christ. Perhaps you have only undergone some religious ritual, like "asking Jesus into your heart," without ever really repenting and believing. The lack of change in your life proves you have not experienced Him, and these doubts are God's way of waking you up to bring you to a living faith.

> *To rest in Christ's finished work is, you see, to be known by Jesus.*

If so, the invitation for you is right now to repent and believe. "Whoever desires," Jesus said, "let him take the water of life freely" (Rev. 22:17). "If you hear His voice, do not harden your heart" (Heb. 4:7).

Assurance Is a Foretaste of Heaven

Assurance is a wonderful thing, perhaps the greatest earthly thing we will ever experience. As Fanny Crosby, that great hymnist of the nineteenth century, said,

> *Blessed assurance, Jesus is mine!*
> *Oh, what a foretaste of glory divine!*
> *Heir of salvation, purchase of God,*
> *Born of His Spirit, washed in His blood.*

> *Perfect submission, perfect delight,*
> *Visions of rapture now burst on my sight;*
> *Angels, descending, bring from above*
> *Echoes of mercy, whispers of love.*

> *Perfect submission, all is at rest,*
> *I in my Savior am happy and blest,*
> *Watching and waiting, looking above,*
> *Filled with His goodness, lost in His love.*

This is my story, this is my song,
Praising my Savior all the day long;
This is my story, this is my song,
Praising my Savior all the day long.

Crosby was physically blind, but her soul had beheld the most beautiful sight of all: the steadfast love of Jesus.

Knowing that you know that you know Jesus, and that Jesus knows you, will lead to more peace and joy than you dreamed possible. It truly is a foretaste of heaven. And when you know for certain that heaven is your inheritance, you'll be moved to radical sacrifice and audacious risk for the kingdom of God. You can give up all you have because you know that in Him you have all that you need.

There was a time in my life when I never thought I'd be able to sing the words "Blessed Assurance, Jesus is Mine" with sincerity. Thank God, I now can. Assurance came to me by understanding more about the gospel. My faith has now found a resting place: *the finished work of Christ.* When the storms of doubt swell up around me, I keep my eyes on Him and His finished work. He is the Rock that holds me above even the waves of my own doubts.

> *Knowing that you know that you know Jesus, and that Jesus knows you, will lead to more peace and joy than you dreamed possible.*

There is One who remains faithful even when we doubt; One who is a firm foundation when our steps falter; One who holds on even when we let go.

Keep your eyes on Him. He is faithful. He said, "It is finished."

WHAT ABOUT BAPTISM?

What do you do about baptism if you think that you might have been "born again" *after* your first one?

There are several answers to this question, depending on your particular situation. If your baptism occurred as an infant, I think the answer is clear: you should be baptized again. Your infant baptism was more a symbol of your parents' faith (and thank God for their faith!) than yours. Every baptism we see in the New Testament, however, was a believer confessing his or her own faith. So be baptized "again," fulfilling the hope your parents had when they baptized you as an infant. Don't fear that you are dishonoring them. What better way to honor the hopes they expressed in your baptism than to choose for yourself to follow Jesus?

But what if you were baptized after an initial conversion experience but now suspect that your actual "regeneration" occurred later? Should you get re-baptized? There's no hard and fast answer, but here's what I'd suggest: if you know *clearly* that you were not saved at the point when you were baptized (i.e., you were pressured into baptism by your parents or friends, had no real grasp on salvation, had some ulterior motive, etc.), then be baptized again.

However, if your baptism depicted the beginning of a journey of faith, a journey marked by numerous "awakenings" and defining moments, let it stand, even if you wonder that perhaps your "regeneration" happened later.

Baptism is postconversion because it symbolizes a public choice to follow Jesus. Thus, to knowingly baptize people who aren't saved yet would pervert and undermine the symbol and its role in the church. But getting the technical order wrong in your own experience is not a perversion of the symbol, it's just a timing mistake—and a minor one, at that.

Baptism is not like the number sequence on a combination lock that if you get out of order will not open. So don't *obsess* about making sure it happened after your regeneration. If you were baptized after making a sincere, conscious confession of faith, accept that and move on, even if you sometimes *suspect* that your regeneration may have happened later. As Christians we continually have new experiences of grace that make us feel like everything we have experienced up to that point was only dimness.

C. S. Lewis describes a day in 1951 (after writing *The Four Loves* and giving the talks that became *Mere Christianity*) where he passed from "mere intellectual acceptance of, to realization of, the doctrine that our sins are forgiven."[1] He did not think of this as his conversion, but he did say that in light of it "what I had previously called 'belief' looked absolutely unreal."[2] *After* writing one of the all-time classics of the Christian faith. When that happens to you, I would encourage you not to see it as conversion, but as a progressive deepening of your relationship with Jesus. God is continuing to mature you in Christ, intellectually, emotionally, and spiritually. Don't get re-baptized.

If you are walking with Jesus now, see your initial confession of Jesus as Lord as the first evidence that God had planted the seed of life in you, even if what you understood then is hardly comparable to what you see now. The validity of our faith is revealed not by the intensity of our first reaction to it, but by our perseverance in it. So, if you are walking with Jesus today, the first sprouts of faith that led to your baptism were likely real ones. Let your first baptism stand.

The writer of Hebrews calls baptism an "elementary" thing that we should build from, not work up to (Heb. 6:1–3). So, unless you *know* you were either completely ignorant or willfully hypocritical at the time of your baptism, get busy with the meatier things of Christianity (i.e., serving Jesus and pouring yourself out for Him)! Move on.

And, if perchance you get to heaven and find out that you were regenerated subsequent to your baptism, it's not like you're going to be demoted to a lesser, "out-of-order-baptism" section in heaven. Baptism is indeed a very important symbol of the faith, a moment in which we identify with Jesus and declare our faith in His finished work to the world. But don't make it more than that.

THE INDISPENSABLE LINK BETWEEN ASSURANCE AND THE DOCTRINE OF JUSTIFICATION BY FAITH ALONE

In this appendix I want to show you why believing salvation comes by faith alone is *essential* to gaining assurance.

In recent years, many Bible-believing Christians have downplayed the doctrine of eternal assurance because they say it creates Christians who believe they can "accept Jesus" and then live however they want. Some say that salvation is, in fact, not received as a gift by faith; it comes, rather, to those who believe *and* do a reasonable job of following Jesus' teachings, to those who live appropriately under the order of His new kingdom and embrace His mission of restoration.[1]

They cite verses such as:

> For not the hearers of the law are just in the sight of God, but the doers of the law will be justified. (Rom. 2:13)

> You see then that a man is justified by works, and not by faith only. (James 2:24)

> And behold, a certain lawyer stood up and tested Him, saying, "Teacher, what shall I do to inherit eternal life?" He said to him, "What is written in the law? What is your reading of it?" So he answered and said, "'You shall love the LORD your God with all your heart, with all your soul, with all your strength, and with all your mind,' and 'your neighbor as yourself.'" And He said to him, "You have answered rightly; do this and you will live." (Luke 10:25–28)[2]

They deny that this equals "salvation by works," because they insist that *(a) our keeping of the law is fueled by God's gracious work in our hearts and (b) because we all fall so far short of the standard we can only hope in Christ's substitutionary work to meets God's standard.* Nonetheless, they insist, we "obtain" Christ's righteousness by keeping the law. To use the Levitical picture we looked at earlier, "good works" are the hand we lay upon the head of Jesus that makes His death our own.

A variation on this common teaching in some Christian circles is that Christ's righteousness is not something God "credits" to our account but something He "infuses" into us. God gives us the grace of wanting to act right, and then evaluates us on the basis of how righteously we act.[3] Salvation is given according to our "good works," though the works themselves are "of grace."

If that is the case, however, I am still left wondering, *How can I know that I've obeyed sufficiently to be counted righteous? Where exactly is the line of demarcation between those who will be damned and those who will be saved?* Or, to ask it perhaps even more clearly: *What level of disobedience disqualifies me from Christ's righteousness?*

Faith most certainly includes an attitude of repentance toward God that expresses itself in good works. *These expressions of faith, however, cannot be confused with faith itself.* Faith's object is Christ and His substitutionary work alone. Saving faith looks *outside* of itself to what Christ has done, not back onto itself at what it has done.

That is the only kind of faith that brings assurance. When we confuse the object of faith with the results of faith, we will soon lose assurance. We will always be plagued by the question, *"Am I doing enough?"* "Enough?" is a question that will drive you to despair. No matter how much you do, the "accuser" will always be crying out for more. You're never "good enough." The good news is that Jesus has done enough. He said it was "finished." So point the accuser there and tell him to shut up.

What, then, do we make of those verses (cited earlier) that seem to imply that salvation is gained by the keeping of the law? Let's take a closer look at them:

> For not the hearers of the law are just in the sight of God,
> but the doers of the law will be justified. (Rom. 2:13)

This verse appears in a section in Romans in which Paul is laying out a case explaining why everyone needs salvation, not explaining how people get saved.

Paul is making two points in this verse. The first is that the Jews' mere possession of the law does not justify them before God, as many Jews seemed to have thought. Of course, if you kept the law perfectly you would be righteous, but merely possessing the law, Paul says, does not make you so. So what Paul says is true: If there is anyone who really does keep the law, they will be justified by it! But no one does. Paul says in the next chapter, *"There is none righteous, no, not one; there is none who understands* (3:10–11). The conclusion of the law is *for all have sinned and fall short of the glory of God"* (3:21–23). Paul's words in 2:13 must therefore be read in light of his conclusion in 3:23: No one can be saved on the basis of obedience to the law. We all fall short.

In another sense, however, Paul is intonating that true faith does produce an internal righteousness that obeys the commands of the law, a conclusion he will flesh out later. The goal of salvation, Paul explains in Romans 12:1–2, is not just forgiveness, but a transformed heart that loves God's laws. Those who have been justified by faith will begin to obey the law from their heart. Where there is no righteous behavior, Paul will say, there has been no heart change. And where there has been no heart change, there has been no salvation.

Keeping the law is not the basis of justification but is the result of it. Faith is the means of salvation; good works are the fruit.[4]

> You see that a person is justified by works and not by faith alone. (James 2:24 ESV)

James isn't contradicting the other writers of the New Testament here by saying that salvation is not by faith alone. Rather, he is saying that the faith that saves will never be alone (that is, alone without good works).

Saving faith, because it is rooted in a new, born-again heart, has in its character the impulses that produce good works. Where those good works are absent, so is saving faith. It's not that good works are equal to, or interchangeable with, faith, but that true faith always produces good works.

Think of faith like a living body. A body that is alive will breathe. Coercing a dead body to breathe by hooking it up to a respirator does not equal making it alive. In the same way, salvation, or life in the soul, happens through faith. But when we are truly alive, we will most certainly "breathe" out good works!

James is not contradicting Paul—in fact, he is assuming the readers already understand and agree with Paul! James is clarifying that the faith that saves is a faith that brings life to the soul, a faith that produces the breath of good works. Where the "breath" of good works is absent, the "life" of faith is also.

And, finally:

> And behold, a certain lawyer stood up and tested Him, saying, "Teacher, what shall I do to inherit eternal life?" He said to him, "What is written in the law? What is your reading of it?" So he answered and said, "'You shall love the LORD your God with all your heart, with all your soul, with all your strength, and with all your mind,' and 'your neighbor as yourself.'" And He said to him, "You have answered rightly; do this and you will live." (Luke 10:25–28)

Was Jesus really saying that we inherit eternal life by loving our neighbor? At first glance it may seem so, but careful attention must be paid to the story that spawned Jesus' answer. Jesus had been asked by a man who had spent his whole life trying to earn eternal life what else he must "do" to secure it.

This was not a seeker earnestly seeking an answer to his question, but a religious man trying to boost his own ego. He did not believe he needed salvation, so Jesus was willing to play his game and beat him on his own terms. He says, "You ask what you must do to inherit eternal life? Easy. *Be perfect.*" I would rephrase Jesus' answer this way: "Seriously? You really believe you have loved God and others well enough to qualify for eternal life?"

Jesus' story reveals the absurdity of the man's boast by exposing the hypocritical heart behind the man's supposedly righteous actions. If you read the entire chapter, you'll see that this is the last guy who should be trying to be saved by keeping the law (he *hated* the Samaritan!). Those who think they have kept the law well will, with a little probing, reveal that their hearts are riddled with inconsistency and hypocrisy. That's what Jesus was doing to this man. He was helping him reckon with the actual state of his heart.

Jesus' words actually serve to reinforce that none of us can possibly hope to be saved through obedience to the law. None of us is loving *enough*. None of us is a *good enough* neighbor. Thus, *if we are to be saved*, it will take more than a renewed commitment to keep the law; more than a new resolve to be better people; more than a greater activism on behalf of the poor. It will take the work of another—another who obeyed the law perfectly in our place and suffered the penalty for our failures. When we believe that He has done that on our behalf, and we rest in that, His righteousness becomes ours.

NOTES

Chapter 1

1. See http://www.barna.org/faith-spirituality/514-barna-study-of-religious-change-since-1991-shows-significant-changes-by-faith-group.

2. Charles H. Spurgeon, "A Free Grace Promise," *Spurgeon's Sermons on Prayer* (Peabody, MA: Hendrickson Publishers, 2007), 140–41.

3. "And therefore, as I suppose many of you are unconverted, and graceless, go home! And away to your closets, and down with your stubborn hearts before God; if you have not done it before, let this be the night. Or do not wait till you go home; begin now, while standing here; pray to God and let the language of your heart be, Lord, convert me! Lord, make me a little child. Lord Jesus, let me not be banished from your kingdom!" George Whitefield, "Marks of a True Conversion," *Sermons of George Whitefield* (Peabody, Mass.: Hendrickson Publishers, 2009), 81.

4. "He [Faithful] bid me go to him and see. Then I said it was presumption. He said, No; for I was invited to come. . . . Then I asked him what I must do when I came; and he told me, I must entreat upon my knees, with all my heart and soul, the Father to reveal Him to me . . . I told him, that I knew not what to say when I came; and he bid me say to this effect: *God be merciful to me a sinner, and make me to know and believe in Jesus Christ; for I see, that if His righteousness had not been, or I have not faith in that righteousness, I am utterly cast away. Lord, I have heard that Thou art a merciful God, and hast ordained that Thy Son Jesus Christ should be the Saviour of the world; and moreover, that Thou art willing to bestow upon such a poor sinner as I am. And I am a sinner indeed. Lord, take therefore this opportunity, and magnify Thy grace in the salvation of my soul, through Thy Son Jesus Christ. Amen.*" John Bunyan, "Hopeful's Conversion," *Pilgrim's Progress* (Grand Rapids, MI: Baker, 1971), 132–33.

Chapter 2

1. See Philippians 3:10.

2. See 1 John 4:19; 2 Corinthians 3:16–18; Galatians 3:2; 5:16–23. The Spirit's power is released in our hearts, Paul explains, as we receive the gospel in faith.

3. See John 14–16. See especially John 16:33.

4. See Isaiah 9:6.

5. See John 10:28–29; Galatians 2:20.

6. Though many have overstated these claims (saying, for example, that Jesus is quoting directly from the *Mishnah* and other Jewish sources, which is not true, or at least cannot be proven), it certainly was customary for the prospective groom to build a "room" onto his father's home (called an *insulae*) to accommodate his new bride. See, for example Ray Vander Laan, Echoes of His Presence (Grand Rapids, MI: Zondervan, 1996), 12–19; Mendell

Lewittes, *Jewish Marriage: Rabbinic Law, Legend, and Custom* (Northvale, NJ: Jason Aronson Inc., 1994), 51–64, 71; Maurice Lamm, *The Jewish Way in Love and Marriage* (San Francisco: Harper & Row, 1980), 154. Furthermore, even if Jesus turns out not to have Jewish wedding procedures in mind in these verses, several other places in John's writing attest to Jesus seeing Himself as the groom and the church as His waiting bride (e.g., John 3:29; Rev. 19:7–9; 21:2; 22:17).

7. See John 15:9.

8. I have written about this extensively in *Gospel: Recovering the Power that Made Christianity Revolutionary* (Nashville: B&H Publishing Group, 2011).

9. Martin Luther, *Lectures on Galatians 1535: Chapters 1–4*, LW 26. Edited by Jaroslav Pelikan. Saint Louis, MO: Concordia Publishing House, 1963. "I am saying this in order to refute the *dangerous doctrine* [perniciosa doctrina, or "damnable doctrine"] of the sophists and the monks, who taught and believed that no one can know for a certainty whether he is in a state of grace, even if he does good works according to his ability and lives a blameless life . . . This *wicked idea*, on which the entire kingdom of the pope rests, is one that you young people should flee and regard with horror as a dangerous plague" (LW 26:377, emphasis added). Also, "Let us thank God, therefore, that we have been delivered from this *monster of uncertainty* [hoc monstro incertitudinis] and that now we can believe for a certainty that the Holy Spirit is crying and issuing that sigh too deep for words in our hearts. And this is our foundation: The Gospel commands us to look, not at our own good deeds or perfections but at God Himself as He promises, and at Christ Himself, the Mediator. By contrast the pope commands us to look, not at God as He promises, not at Christ our High Priest, but at our own works and merits. From the latter course, doubt and despair necessarily follow; but from the former, certainty and the joy of the Spirit" (LW 26:386–387, emphasis added).

10. See 1 John 4:19.

11. The original source of this story has been difficult to track down. Bryan Chappell references it in his *Christ-Centered Preaching*. Through a personal correspondence, Chappell told me that he has since lost the original citation, though he remembered reading it in the collection of John Bunyan's letters kept at Oxford University.

12. E.g., John 3:16, 36; 9:36–38.

Chapter 3

1. I'll explain more in chapter 5 about the difference between saving belief and a merely intellectual assent which even the demons give to Jesus.

2. New Testament scholar J. Ramsey Michaels says, "While the contrast with 'whoever believes in the Son' (v. 36a) makes clear that the meaning is the same, the change of verb helps define 'believing' as obedience, or 'coming to the Light' (compare vv. 20–21), rather than mere intellectual assent." *The Gospel of John*, The New International Commentary on the New Testament (Grand Rapids, MI: Wm. B. Eerdmans Publishing Co., 2010), 227. The Greek word in question *apeithon*, is translated elsewhere as "disobey" (Rom. 2:8 HCSB). In John 3:36, the KJV, NKJV, and HCSB use "believe" for both clauses; the NIV opts for "believe" in the first and "rejects" in the second; the ESV, ASV, and RSV use variants of "disobey" in the second.

3. Inspiration for this illustration comes from Tim Keller preaching a sermon on Hebrews 7:17–27 at Redeemer Presbyterian in New York City in 2005. Keller credits Dick Lucas as its source.

4. Note that I am not trying to imply that the Father wants one thing and Jesus another. Jesus is the Word of the Father, which means He perfectly expresses the heart of God. What Jesus feels, the Father feels. I am simply illustrating that no claim against us can stand. If anything, it would be more accurate to say that Satan is the one who stands before the Father accusing us.

5. See 1 John 1:9; Matthew 26:39.

6. See John 19:30; Romans 4:25; Hebrews 1:3.

7. See John 14:6; Acts 4:12.

8. The first mention of such a practice comes in a thirteenth-century Rabbinic commentary called *Zohar*, Volume 16, "Emor"; Section 34, "Yom Kippur"; Paragraph 251 (p. 255), though it seems to be loosely based on Exodus 28:33–35. Jewish leaders had been known to add provisions to the Mosaic laws to make sure that they kept them. Whether or not this was one of them at the time of Zechariah cannot be known for sure. What is certain is that entering the Holy of Holies was a serious, life-threatening endeavor.

9. Tim Keller, quoting Ray Dillard from a sermon he heard Dillard preach, in *King's Cross: The Story of the World in the Life of Jesus* (New York: Penguin Group, 2011), 79–80. For more on this, see Jacob Milgrom, *Leviticus 1–16*, The Anchor Bible, 1015–16. Milgrom draws his conclusions from the Mishnah that expands on Yom Kippur with most detail, the *Yoma*. The *Yoma* includes details such as appointing a backup priest in case the first is unfit, "dry runs" in which the priest practices the motions of pouring the blood, and the specific order of body parts to bathe.

10. Keller, *King's Cross*, 81.

11. See Ephesians 5:22–31.

12. See 2 Corinthians 5:21. I have to give credit to my friend David Platt for a little inspiration here. He fleshes this analogy out better than anyone I've ever heard!

13. "The Solid Rock," public domain.

Chapter 4

1. See http://www.newsmax.com/InsideCover/poll-americans-believe-christ/2010/04/04/id/354704.

2. Martin Luther, *Commentary on Romans* (Grand Rapids: Kregel, 1954), 147–48, emphasis added.

3. Martin Luther, *Commentary on Galatians*, from the preface, xvii–xx. In *The Crossway Classic Commentary Series*, ed. Alister McGrath and J. I. Packer (Wheaton: Crossway, 1998).

4. See Appendix 2, "The Indispensable Link Between Assurance and the Doctrine of Justification by Faith Alone."

Chapter 5

1. C. S. Lewis, *Mere Christianity* (New York: Harper Collins, 1952), 56.

2. See also Acts 3:19 and Acts 26:20.

3. See Mark 5:25–34; Luke 22:31–34; John 21:1–19; John 20:24–29.

4. See James 2:26.

5. Flannery O'Connor, *Wise Blood: A Novel* (New York: Farrar, Straus, and Giroux, 1949), 22.

6. See 1 John 3:6.

7. Jared Wilson, *Gospel Wakefulness* (Wheaton: Crossway, 2011), 207.

8. As noted in chapter 1, see Paul's confrontation of Peter in Galatians 2:11–14.

9. See 2 Corinthians 12:7.

10. See Luke 23:50–51; John 19:38.

11. See Mark 9:22–24.

12. See, for example, Luke 6:46; 14:26, 33.

13. I have written on the demands the gospel makes of our lives in *Gospel: Recovering the Power that Made Christianity Revolutionary* (Nashville: B&H, 2011). Embracing the gospel leads inevitably to a life of worship, generosity, and mission.

14. The first of the Ten Commandments was, of course, that we worship, seek and serve God like nothing else on earth.

15. See Hebrews 2:3; 4:1, 7; Revelation 22:17; Matthew 23:37.

16. See John 1:12–13; Philippians 2:13.

17. Charles Spurgeon, *The Soul Winner* (New Kensington, PA: Whitaker House, 1995), 23.

18. See 1 Peter 1:22–25; Matthew 13:31–32.

19. See John 15:4–5.

20. See Ephesians 3:20–21.

21. N. T. Wright, *Matthew for Everyone*, Part 1 (London: SPCK, 2002), 19–22.

22. Letter to Bethlehem Baptist Church, April 19, 2006. http://www.desiringgod.org/resource-library/taste-see-articles/thoughts-on-jesus-demand-to-repent.

Chapter 6

1. In that the Bible is not just the word of man, but also the word of God, it cannot contradict itself. God cannot change His mind or go back on His perspective (2 Tim. 3:16–17; Ps. 119:89).

2. For example, the writer of Hebrews also teaches that salvation is a gift purchased once and for all by Christ, given to us an "eternal covenant" by God's "unchangeable purpose" and "unchangeable oath," and that Jesus will "never leave us nor forsake us." The writer urges us to hold fast to the "sure and steadfast anchor of our souls" (Heb. 6:17–19; 9:26; 13:5, 20–21). Peter T. O'Brien, author of *The Epistle to the Hebrews in The Pillar New Testament Commentary Series,* says, "Even within Hebrews itself there are powerful words of encouragement and assurance based on God's faithfulness to fulfill his promises to his people (Heb. 2:10; 6:10–20), and so because of the finality of Christ's sacrifice (Heb. 9:11–28; 10:14–18)." See http://thegospel-coalition.org/blogs/tgc/2012/01/09/warning-passages-ahead.

3. I gained much help in this section from the following: D. A. Carson, "Reflections on Assurance," in *Still Sovereign: Contemporary Perspectives on Election, Foreknowledge, and Grace,* ed. by Thomas R. Schreiner and Bruce A. Ware (Grand Rapids: Baker, 2000), 247–76; C.

Adrian Thomas, *A Case for Mixed-Audience with Reference to the Warning Passages in the Book of Hebrews* (New York: Lang, 2008), 184–85; *Four Views on the Warning Passages in Hebrews*, ed. by H. W. Bateman (Grand Rapids: Kregel, 2007), 172–219; Thomas R. Schreiner and Ardel B. Caneday, *The Race Set Before Us: A Biblical Theology of Perseverance and Assurance* (Downers Grove, IL: Intervarsity Press, 2001); and, a talk given by Tom Schreiner at the 2011 Resurgence conference in Seattle, WA, entitled, *"Being Sure about Being Saved, Parts 1–2"*: http://theresurgence.com/2011/12/04/being-sure-about-being-saved; http://theresurgence.com/2011/12/11/being-sure-about-being-saved-part-2.

4. In the writer's "congregation" there is undoubtedly a mixture of both genuine and insincere believers, such as you would find in any church congregation. This is not to imply that we allow known unbelievers to function as members in a church, but that there is often simply no way to know who is truly saved and who is posing. See C. Adrian Thomas, *A Case for Mixed-Audience with Reference to the Warning Passages in the Book of Hebrews* (New York: Lang, 2008), 184–85. Peter O'Brien says, "It is evident that some had been truly converted and had genuinely appropriated Christ's saving work for themselves. How many and who they all were, the author does not know exactly. But he addresses the whole congregation on the basis of what he has observed, and urges them to hold firmly to their confession of faith in Christ, their Christian hope without wavering, and their confidence in God (Heb. 3:6, 14; Heb. 4:14; Heb. 6:18; Heb. 10:23). Significantly, even when the author refers to those who commit apostasy he uses the third person plural rather than the second (e.g., 'those *who* have once been enlightened . . . and *who* have fallen away,' Heb. 6:4–6), and does not explicitly identify them with his listeners. Though some are apparently in great danger he does not assert that they have committed apostasy. The warnings, like the divine promises, are intended to prevent this from happening." See http://thegospelcoalition.org/blogs/tgc/2012/01/09/warning-passages-ahead.

5. See Mark 4:16–19.

6. See Luke 9:62.

7. Compare Genesis 20:2–6.

8. See John 6:35–39.

9. Luke 12:10. See also John 6:66; 2 Peter 3:17; Hebrews 10:26–29, 39; and 2 Thessalonians 2:11. Paul said that his blasphemous rejection of God's salvation was done "ignorantly in unbelief" (1 Tim. 1:13). He recognized that there is a stubborn hardness of heart that can drive God's Spirit away permanently.

10. Ed Welch notes that the charge is made against religious *leaders* who were unwavering in the blasphemy and opposition to Jesus, even after being convinced He possessed divine authority. Welch has written a good, concise, pastoral article analyzing the passages in question at http://www.ccef.org/unpardonable-sin.

11. See Philippians 2:12–13; 1 Corinthians 12:3; John 6:44.

12. See Revelation 22:17; John 6:37.

13. See Hebrews 3:15.

14. See Luke 3:8; Jeremiah 31:33–35; Ezekiel 36:26.

15. Wayne Grudem, *Bible Doctrines* (Grand Rapids, MI: Zondervan, 1999), 336.

16. See 2 Peter 1:10; Philippians 2:12–13.

17. See Philippians 2:12.

18. *Synod of Dort,* 5:13. Article 14 says, "And, just as it has pleased God to begin this work of grace in us by the proclamation of the gospel, so he preserves, continues, and completes his work by the hearing and reading of the gospel, by meditation on it, by its exhortations, threats, and promises."

19. "Come Thou Fount of Every Blessing," 1758. Words by Robert Robinson.

20. See Thomas R. Schreiner and Ardel B. Caneday, *The Race Set Before Us: A Biblical Theology of Perseverance and Assurance* (Downers Grove, IL: InterVarsity Press, 2001). Again, this chapter owes much to his work and insight in that book.

21. See 2 Timothy 2:13.

Chapter 7

1. See 1 Corinthians 1:18.

2. See 2 Corinthians 2:16.

3. See Titus 3:5.

4. Romans 7:21–23.

5. I know most of you don't have a lot of extra talents stuffed into your wallets, so it may be hard to get your mind around how much money that is—think, "the national debt." Some scholars say that a single talent was more than ten years' wages for the average man. Furthermore, "ten thousand" was the highest number in Greek, so to use it was like saying "infinity." In other words, this man owed the other an infinite debt he could never hope to pay off.

6. Paul says, "I find it to be a law that when I want to do right, evil lies close at hand" (Rom. 7:21 ESV). The apostle John, after explaining that true believers are no longer held captive by sin, says, "If we say that we have no sin, we deceive ourselves, and the truth is not in us"; and, "If anyone sins, we have an Advocate with the Father, Jesus Christ the righteous" (1 John 1:8; 2:1).

7. Again, reflect on 1 John 1:8–9, or Paul's statement in 1 Timothy 1:15 that he was the "chief" of sinners." He felt that way probably because God's grace had illuminated his heart to see how sinful it really was.

8. Mike McKinley, *Am I Really a Christian* (Wheaton: Crossway, 2011), 38–39, 72. John Bunyan, who struggled for many years to gain assurance, made the same point in book 2 of *Pilgrim's Progress.* Bunyan was one prone to an overly pessimistic view of himself. It was others in his local church in Bedfordshire who helped him see the evidences of God's grace at work in him. He depicts this in book 2 of *Pilgrim's Progress,* in which the pilgrims are able to see the new beauty shining out of one another but not for themselves: "When the women were this adorned, they seemed to be a terror one to the other; for that they could not see that glory each one had on herself, which they could see in each other. Now therefore they began to esteem each other better than themselves. For, 'You are fairer than I am,' said one; and, 'You are more comely than I am,' said another." (John Bunyan, *Pilgrims Progress*, Grand Rapids, MI: Baker, 1971, 199–200).

Chapter 8

1. See Romans 4:5; Galatians 3:1–3; John 7:38.

2. See James 4:8. C. S. Lewis, *Mere Christianity,* 122. Peter Kreeft says, "God often withholds from us the grace to avoid a lesser sin because we are in danger of a greater sin. To

avoid pride, he sometimes lets us fall into lust, since lust is usually obvious, undisguised, and temporary, while pride is not." See *Back to Virtue* (San Francisco: Ignatius Press, 1992), 168.

3. Adapted from Michael Reeves, *The Unquenchable Flame,* (Nashville: B&H, 2010), 175. I took the liberty of updating some of Bunyan's language to make Bunyan's statement more understandable to modern readers. I do not believe I altered any of Bunyan's original intent.

4. "But he can never say to me. 'I never knew you,' for he has known me as his poor dependent, a beggar for years at his door. . . . Thou knowest me, Lord, for I came to thee, and said, God be merciful to me a sinner . . . Dost thou ask me who I am? 'Once a sinner near despair, I sought thy mercy seat by prayer.'" From "The Ploughman," in *Farm Sermons.* See http://www.spurgeon.org/misc/plough.htm. At the end, Spurgeon is quoting hymn writer John Newton, http://www.preceptaustin.org/spurgeon_on_matthew.htm.

Appendix 1

1. Jared Wilson, *Gospel Wakefulness* (Wheaton: Crossway, 2011), 186. From *Collected Letters of C. S. Lewis, Volume III* (San Francisco, CA: Harper, 2007), 425.

2. Ibid., 425, 935.

Appendix 2

1. For example, N. T. Wright says, "I repeat what I have always said: that the final justification . . . will be pronounced over the totality of the life lived." N. T. Wright, "Justification: Yesterday, Today, and Forever," *Journal of the Evangelical Theological Society* 54, no. 1 (March 2011): 49–63. Even M. Scot McKnight, a frequent contributor to marquee evangelical publications such as *Christianity Today,* is opaque on the issue: "I see a tendency, which seems to me to be a subtle attempt to let the Reformation have too much influence on exegesis, to prefer this formula: faith is *demonstrated* by works. . . . Yes, works demonstrate faith, but they also perfect and fulfill faith . . . the two work together to produce a working faith that saves" (Scot McKnight, *The Letter of James. The New International Commentary on the New Testament* [Grand Rapids, MI: William B. Eerdmans Publishing Company, 2011], 244, emphasis original).

2. This was the conversation that preceded Jesus' telling of the parable of the Good Samaritan.

3. See, for example, *Catechism of the Catholic Church,* section 1856. Catholic theologian Richard McBrien states: "Because of this inner transformation, the human person is now capable of meritorious actions that are at once initiated by God's grace but also fully human," (Richard P. McBrien, *Catholicism: New Edition* [New York: HarperCollins Publishers, 1994], 179). See also *Canons and Decrees of the Council of Trent: English Translation,* translated by H. J. Schroeder (Rockford, IL: Tan Books and Publishers, Inc., 1978), session 6, chapter 9, 11, 16; canon 9 and 24.

4. See Romans 1:17; 4:5.

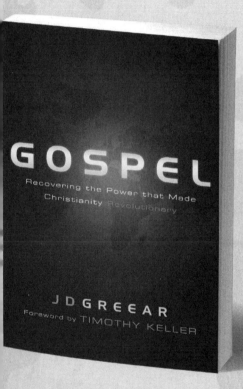